THROUGH THE STORM

THE PRICE OF FAME

CHANTEL DEAN

13TH & JOAN

Through the Storm: The Price of Fame. Copyright 2025 by Chantel Dean.

All rights reserved. No part of this publication may be reproduced, distributed, or transmitted in any form or by any means, including photocopying, recording, or other electronic or mechanical methods, without the prior written permission of the publisher, except in the case of brief quotations embodied in critical reviews and certain other noncommercial uses permitted by copyright law.

For permission requests, write to the publisher, addressed "Attention: Permissions Coordinator," 205 N. Michigan Avenue, Suite #810, Chicago, IL 60601. 13th & Joan books may be purchased for educational, business or sales promotional use. For information, please email the Sales Department at sales@13thandjoan.com.

Printed in the U. S. A.

First Printing, August 2025

Library of Congress Cataloging-in-Publication Data has been applied for.

ISBN: 978-1-961863-89-7

This book is dedicated to my grandmother,
Lanie T. Frazier, and my great-grandparents,
Ruth Davis and Pastor John W. Davis.

The seeds you planted and the prayers you prayed were not in vain.

To my Baltimore School for the Arts Ensemble:
I love you all deeply and beyond measure.

Contents

Introduction: Prepare for the Storm 1
Chapter 1: When The Rain Starts............................... 10
Chapter 2: Navigating the Storm 28
Chapter 3: Unexpected Downpours........................... 45
Chapter 4: Misty Rain 61
Chapter 5: The Living Water.. 77
Chapter 6: The Rain of My Tears 91
Chapter 7: The Scattered Showers of My Dreams.... 107
Chapter 8: The Torrent of a Pandemic 123
Chapter 9: Silent Rain 139
Chapter 10: After the Storm 156
Conclusion: The Rainbow.. 172
About the Author 181

INTRODUCTION

Prepare for the Storm

VICTORY AFTER THE STORM.

— Chantel Dean

As we learn and grow, our elders tend to play the biggest roles in our lives. These are your parents, grandparents, aunts, and uncles. Most children are raised in the home with their parents and can envision where they will be in the years to come. My life was quite different. I was raised by my great-grandparents because it was a better environment for me. They taught me how to be a young lady and love God. I knew from a young age what I wanted to be, or so I thought. I worked so hard to become a Hollywood actress and have my name in the credits. All of my friends were in the arts, and it seemed like it would be the best place for me. What I didn't realize was there were things that I would have to go through to achieve that dream.

I moved from my hometown, Washington, D.C., to the big city of Los Angeles to pursue the role of a lifetime. Chantel in full action. I thought that if I stayed there long enough, everything would work out fine. I was in the place where the stars were born. After being in a film, my eyes were wide open to what filming and being around great actors felt like. Seeing myself on screen was the victory at the end of the war, and I wanted to taste more of it.

I thought going to a performing arts school would place me in the right places to be seen. I would perfect my craft so that I could stand out among the others. All I needed to do was get there and everything would fall into place. As a teenager, I had it all planned out. I followed all the rules, listened to my guardians, and attended church. After being accepted into school, I just knew Los Angeles was meant to be. I would see my name in lights and return home a celebrity. My family would be so proud of me because I accomplished my goals.

In the movies, they say that fame costs. I didn't know the price would be so high. Throughout my time trying to be what I wanted, I was always chasing that dream. You hear about people running after their dreams, but I never understood what they meant. Being an actress always seemed to be bolting in the other direction. I would catch up to it, and when I thought I had it, the dream would tease me and keep going. It was a carrot that was always dangled in front of me to keep me in a place that I had outgrown. Right when I was ready to give up and move into my purpose, there was that carrot. It was right in my face but so far away. I tried so hard to grasp it, but it seemed to be letting me know I was going the wrong way. The storm was up ahead, and I needed to turn around. I never listened. I fought harder because I had come too far to give up. I lost too much to go back home without it. The carrot was going to be mine.

Sometimes what we want for ourselves and what God wants for us are two different things. We work so hard for what we want. We stay in places too long, whether that be in relationships, friendships, jobs, or places we live. God may have called you to move two months ago, but your stubbornness and pride kept you struggling in a one-bedroom apartment instead of thriving in the five-bedroom home He had waiting for you. God has the best strategy. Although we may not see it, He does. If you trust Him and lean not to your own understanding, everything will work out for you.

It took me years of following after a career instead of God to learn that.

Your gifts will bring you in front of exceptional people, but that doesn't mean you are supposed to stay there. I met great men and women, some millionaires and others who lived paycheck to paycheck. Some had huge hearts and others were ruthless. There were so many lessons I acquired from all of those people—learning how to spend, save, live, be cultured, forgive, share, love, and when to let go. Letting go is the most formidable because it is the hardest thing to do. Some people are only with you for a short amount of time and push you toward destiny. They open doors for you and get you in the correct rooms. The rooms can be a job, a home, cars, and a host of other things. They aren't meant to be lifelong connections, they get you from point A to point B. They are hard to lose but bring so much joy to you while they are present.

Blessings are waiting for you on the other side of the pain and the loss. My advice is to endure the test given to you and build up your strength and resilience. People are fickle and will come and go, but you have to press on. Never stop going, and keep God first. Through every problem that arose in my life while on my way to my destiny, I never forgot about God. He always had a plan for me. When I needed Him, I would call on Him.

He always answered me in ways that I could not imagine. I saw Him do the impossible on my behalf. Every time I was low and in a weary state of mind, He showed me who He was. All I had to do was seek Him.

When your dreams start to become a nightmare, sometimes you don't know where to turn. You find that you have neglected family and friends for your own selfish endeavors. The people you met, whom you thought cared, are not who they appeared to be. They used you to get ahead and threw the relationship away when they were finished. You can find yourself in a state of sadness and depression because your support system is nonexistent. When this happens, remember to encourage yourself in the Lord. Even if your situation does not change overnight, it will soon. God sees every night you cried yourself to sleep and every morning you awoke to find nothing had changed. God's timing is perfect.

Life brings with it many storms. In those storms, we learn more about who we are and what we can handle. Storms come to bring an abundance of rain for our plants to grow. The issue is, an overflow of water can be harmful in the wrong places. Storms bring thunder. Its sound is to help prevent us from staying in a place that we need to leave before the lightning strikes. After all of this, once the storm has passed, the waters succeed and the grass is beautiful. Clouds have moved away, and the sun pierces through the gorgeous blue sky.

Science has a way of always intertwining in our lives. God created all things, so it makes sense that it does. Overflow of rain can be a blessing or a curse when you aren't prepared. When it comes to the ground, there are things in place so the water can run back out to the rivers and oceans. If dams and barriers are not in place, the overflow causes flooding. It keeps people indoors or stuck in a place if they are outside. Now, place yourself in that same situation. God can overflow your finances, but if you are not a good steward, you lose them quickly. There are financial classes set up to help you, but if you don't take them, you won't be prepared. You will spend all that you have and the inheritance meant for you to invest for future generations.

The best thing to do is learn the types of storms you are in and always remember, storms pass. They don't come to stay. Recognize that you are prepared for the storm, and you can outlast it. Find your purpose in the storms of life. I thought I was supposed to be a big-time actress. I tried out and was hired as an extra more than once but not enough to form a career. In hindsight, I was supposed to meet artistic people and move around the United States. Every place I lived changed me. My testimony and character were built through my experiences. I was bold to make the moves I did at such a young age. Many people won't leave home in pursuit of destiny. My pick-up-and-go mentality led me straight into storms. It wasn't close to what I had in mind, but just what God had for me. I helped others going through similar experiences.

In the midst of my storm, I couldn't see past the rain. I gained wisdom through the process. When you are living day-to-day and trying to figure out how you are going to eat and pay your bills, it's hard to trust anybody. You are in the life that you made for yourself, and then you look up, and you are desperate. You don't want to tell anybody the truth of your situation because of how you will be perceived. You were supposed to make it out. You were supposed to be the first in the family to make it to the NFL or graduate school. Everyone is relying on you to break the generational curse. The weight is on your shoulders, and you can't stomach letting them know that you need help. They are going through their own storms. How dare you ask them to assist you?

God has a way to humble you and let you know that you will still be that person for the family. His promise will still stand in your life for your calling. There are people willing to be there for you, if you allow them. Go to God because He is a safe place, and He will send you what you need to get you through. God allowed me to position myself in all the careers I wanted. I was able to see people, places, and things I didn't even pray for. God has a permissive will and a perfect will. His permissiveness let me do what I wanted, but His perfection allowed me to be who He wanted. The version of me that He saw was so much greater than the person I was.

I wrote this memoir after years of telling my story in bits and pieces. The ongoing emotion I found others to have was shock. From my outward appearance, I didn't look like what I had been through. They couldn't believe I had gone through so much. Every time this happened there was a nudging of the Holy Spirit for me to tell my testimony. I could see how it affected others and how they wanted to know more. My lessons were helping others to get through their storms.

In this season of life, I am focusing on building my ministry, furthering my education, and touching the lives of others. This book is one way I want to further my reach. I want you to know that after the storm, you will be greater because you were able to endure. Your foundation is strong enough to withstand your life's storm. You will see clearly what you are supposed to do, and your past will be washed away. It happened to you, but it didn't break you. No one is going to be there to always pick you up. Encourage yourself in God because He loves you. Your story is as important as anyone else's, and no one will ever know the depth of what you dealt with if you don't tell them. You got out, and you can help someone else do the same. Lastly, remember to hold on and fight. You will make it through the storm.

CHAPTER 1

When The Rain Starts

MAKE SURE TO HAVE AN UMBRELLA.
— Chantel Dean

WHEN YOU ARE YOUNG, YOU HAVE MANY dreams. You attend high school with a goal of who you want to be. You are full of light and joy because you have imagined it. Then, you begin to touch and taste it. It is the most exciting thing in your life and all you speak about. No one can stop you from pursuing it. I remember that feeling like it was yesterday.

My first day at Baltimore School for the Arts was

one of excitement. I wore an off-the-shoulder top and walked through the doors, breaking barriers as I was accepted as a senior, which is unheard of. I walked into The Tupac Shakur Black Box Theatre for a roll call of all the theatre students. I was placed in the junior ensemble for my theatre training. I stood before my class and sang "Somewhere Over the Rainbow" as our musical theatre teacher, Becky Mossing, instructed the ensemble.

My dream was to be a movie star, to be on the big screen alongside all the great actors and actresses. Then, it happened, my moment. It was my major project. Tyler Perry was filming for the movie *Daddy's Little Girls*. I was an extra, and I was able to be closer to the celebrities. During filming, I sat next to Louis Gossett Jr., a legend. I couldn't believe it. Little ole me, right there next to this actor who had been in the business for years. The cherry on top was what he said to me.

As I sat on the wooden seats of Ebenezer Baptist Church in Atlanta waiting for the cameras to roll, he told me, "You are so beautiful no one will be looking at me."

I was thankful for the compliment and immediately said, "Thank you, sir." He was a gentleman and a great person to film with. He made us all feel at ease and built confidence in us that we were where we should be. My heart was so joyful because of that.

He wasn't the only famous person I was in contact with. I sat behind Idris Elba in another scene. He had the same presence as Louis Gosset Jr. Sometimes, extras have scenes where they just walk in the background and don't get that close, but I was the exception. I could only think of God opening this door to my dream, which fueled me to pursue this career in entertainment. This wasn't my big break. I wasn't getting calls for being in the movie, but it paved the way for my goal of making it in the business. I even got a signed movie poster from Tyler Perry. The movie came out in 2007, and I was a part of that moment.

By the summer of 2008, I had just graduated from Baltimore School for the Arts. I was seventeen years old and felt the world was at my fingertips. I applied and was accepted to the American Musical and Dramatic Academy, an acting and dance school in Los Angeles. I had a movie under my belt and a beat in my heart. It was time to move to the next phase of my life. My dad dropped me off in my dorm room at The American Musical Dramatic Academy in Hollywood. We had only been fully involved in each other's lives for one year. This happened after the tragic suicide of my stepmother and the death of my primary guardian, Grandma Lanie. I grew up as a preacher's kid in a Christian home with my great-grandparents and their daughter. I always had a quite rocky relationship with my parents, and they gave little to no financial help.

My father, who had a restaurant in the '90s with Denzel Washington and Lakers Legend Norm Nixon, took me to lunch with Norm Nixon at a quaint restaurant the day before he dropped me off in Santa Monica. At that lunch, Norm Nixon advised me to stay focused in California. The next day, my dad gave me $40 and said don't do anything I wouldn't do. As he drove off from my dorm, from that moment, I was on my own to figure out life.

My dorm room was average, which was enough for me. I turned my tiny walk-in closet into an office. I started adjusting to my new surroundings but knew I would need transportation to get to certain places, like the grocery store or around the city for casting calls. My great-grandparents on my mom's side, Pastor John Davis and Ruth Davis, had given me $2,000 as a graduation present. I was still a teenager, but I was mature enough to know that I should buy a used car because it would be affordable. I didn't have much time to look around and debate about the type of car I would like. I knew very little about purchasing a vehicle, and it showed. The dealer must have seen how green I was from a mile away. I told them how much money I had to spend on a car. From what was on the lot, an old white Ford Taurus caught my eye, and I purchased my first car in my new city.

The car began to have issues as soon as I left the lot. I unknowingly acquired a lemon. The car battery would die consistently. Not understanding that this should not be happening and having no one to ask, I continued driving it. I wanted to learn my way around. How else would I do that without a car? It may not have been perfect, but it was mine and took me from point A to point B.

Two weeks passed, and I attended classes and began socializing with other students. I was fitting in and enjoying my new atmosphere. One of my classmates invited me to a party, but I wasn't sure about going. I would be alone because there was no one to take with me but on the other hand, it was a chance for me to meet more people. It was a hard decision because the party scene was never my thing. I valued God, church, family, and friends. I knew that partying went along with drinking and smoking, all the things that I stayed away from. This new place in California was different. I was free and able to go places. So many things were available to me, and no one was there to reprimand me or give me sound advice. I realized I was on my own, and all decisions were on me.

The party was in Long Beach, a car ride away. I arrived to what I thought the gathering would be—a sea of people listening to music and drinking. I tried to stay and blend in, but I stood out like a sore thumb. I didn't look like I belonged and felt as though I didn't. I hung around for a while but left around midnight. I got in my car and started driving back on the 405 freeway in the fast lane. Suddenly, my car stopped moving. It completely shut down in the middle of the road. I reached for any light to warn others that I was there, but not even my hazard lights would turn on. Panic set in because no one could see me. It was the middle of the night and pitch black outside. Getting out of the car wasn't an option because the traffic was so bad. My clothes didn't glow in the dark, nor did I. No one would see me walking until they were close enough to hit me. I did the only thing I knew to do in a time of trouble. I spoke to my Heavenly Father.

I put my hands on the steering wheel and began to pray.

"Heavenly Father, save me. Don't let me die here. Keep the cars away from me. Help me, God."

I was certain that in order to get out of the situation, I would be in an accident. There were no other possibilities because so many cars were swerving, blowing their horns, and not seeing me until the last minute. Leaving earth at that moment was all I could envision. This was my last day, and my death was because of a lemon car I drove to a party. I should have stayed in my dorm room. My prayers began to work because God brought something to my attention. At that instance, I remembered

I could call 911. I fidgeted with my phone until I could dial the number. The operator answered and could hear the constant horns blowing in the background through the phone and my crying.

In between sobs, I screamed, "I am going to die!"

The operator advised me to stay with them on the line and tried their hardest to calm me down. It was a task even they couldn't do. They asked for my location, and I explained that I was on the 405 freeway. I looked in the rearview mirror knowing that they wouldn't make it in time to help me. I watched as every headlight came an inch closer to killing me. My tears wouldn't stop.

With every vehicle that veered off, I thanked God but to myself said, "This is it, you're going to die."

In the blink of an eye, I saw an Isuzu truck going faster than the other cars. It was moving so rapidly that I knew it was the one. I turned around and grabbed the wheel. The impact caused my car to spin and slide a hundred feet. I was screaming at the top of my lungs as the car slammed into the median strip. When the movement stopped, I noticed hundreds of cars behind me and smoke rising from the hood of mine.

I was alive! The nightmare was over, but I couldn't open the door to leave. It was crushed. I had to think fast as glass covered my body, and the car may have caught on fire. I climbed out of my front window when I heard a man yelling that he was a doctor. I wept because I'd never been in a car accident before. I checked my skin, but there were no scratches on me by the grace of God. '

I was on my way over to the other car saying, "Please, God, let whoever is in that car be okay."

Trembling, I walked closer to her passenger door. I saw her as she stumbled out of the vehicle, and we were both overcome by emotions.

I kept apologizing because of the guilt that my car shut down. If I could have picked the car up and moved it, I would have. The phrase 'I am sorry' escaped my lips countless times. As we stood there still in shock, law enforcement pulled up. To my surprise, they made the other driver take a breathalyzer test. The next thing I knew, she was getting arrested and put into the backseat of a police car. More guilt tugged at me knowing she was under the influence of alcohol. Soon after, the police offered me a ride back to my dorm, and I accepted. As I went into my room, it was early the next morning. I had lost my car and almost died. The first few weeks of my new life were slowly turning in the wrong direction.

I continued my classes but was beginning to struggle through school. I was starving. My groceries were slowly running out, and I didn't have a meal plan. My bank account was dry. Being unable to buy food or things you need is a huge distraction in school. Imagine trying to focus on a task or listening to teachers while your stomach is growling. Being unable to get the essentials for your body or the paper you need because you don't have any income is beyond discouraging. I looked at who would be able to lend me some finances. My great-grandparents spent their entire lives raising me. I didn't want to burden them with any of my problems. They had done enough. I used their money to purchase that horrible car. I resorted to calling my dad and asked if he could put some money in my account. I wasn't sure what answer I would get because he did bring me there. Maybe our relationship was mended enough that he would support me. He replied that I had another parent and should contact them. Nothing had changed. My mom, who suffered from bipolar schizophrenia, was in no position to help me financially. I was stuck with no money and no one to ask for help.

I made the choice to leave school because I was broke. My choice was to either go to rehearsals after class on an empty stomach or get a full-time job. I chose to work. I could get back into school once I picked myself back up. Going back home was not for me. I came to L.A. to be an actress, and I wasn't going to leave without accomplishing my goal. Within a few weeks, I was moving into my first studio apartment. It was a special day. November 4, 2008, my eighteenth birthday. My place was in Hollywood's heart at 1842 N Cherokee Avenue, Apartment 409. I had a residence but no clarity on my next steps. I still had no vehicle and all my finances went straight to pay my bills. Everything I needed required income. It was time for a change. I submitted a few more job applications and finally received a phone call back.

I was hired as a dishwasher for a Jamaican restaurant for a few weeks. It was too far to walk but only a few bus rides from where I lived. Being alone took a toll on me. I had no assistance because although I socialized with others while at school, true relationships were not created. Once I left school, I was forgotten about. I kept getting lost trying to figure out which bus was the correct one to take. Memorizing the schedules and bus stops was harder than I thought. I was soon fired. One day I had a job, and the next, it was gone due to my lack of knowledge of the public transportation system. There are only so many times a supervisor will hear, "I'm late because I missed my bus." They may have thought I was just a liar who didn't want to work.

As I continued to look for other jobs and get my head together, I was ultimately served an eviction notice from my apartment. At that point, I was shattered. My life was collapsing around me. I had about two dollars in my pocket, and they were all quarters. The city was closing in on me fast, and I needed to breathe. I went around the corner to a place called Tommy's. I loved to get an order of their chili fries. I wanted something familiar, and that restaurant gave me comfort. I knew I couldn't afford anything on the menu, but I still went inside. I approached the register and immediately started crying. I was so hungry and hopeless. All I wanted was a hot meal. A man standing behind me in line saw my reaction. I firmly believe this man was an angel. He ended up covering my food cost and kindly asked me to sit down with him.

As we sat in each other's company, he asked me what was happening with me. I mentioned the mishaps I was experiencing since my move. I told him about how I got in a car accident with no insurance and lost my job because it was too far away. He said he knew someone who could assist me and took me to an office at 8383 Wilshire Boulevard. He dropped me off, then disappeared like an angel would. I went in, not knowing who I was going to see. A woman asked what I needed, and I told her that a man dropped me off because I was in an accident. The woman, whose name was Mildred, turned out to be an outstanding secretary.

She told me, "We don't take anyone who doesn't have insurance. He's a very busy lawyer. He only sees million-dollar cases, but I'll see if I can squeeze you in."

He only sees million-dollar clients. Who was this man? I had no idea where I was or who he was. I didn't have a million dollars. I barely had two dollars and no alternatives. I had no choice but to sit there and wait. What was going to come out of this? I didn't know. What I knew was an angel brought me there, so I was right where God wanted me to be.

Two hours passed while I sat thinking about life and how I ended up there. The door finally opened, and a prestigious lawyer came out. His name was J. Shaffer Smith. He asked me to come into his office. I sat and told him what happened and that I didn't have any insurance. I had only been in L.A. for a few months before this car wreck. I should have died in it from the way I was living now.

He said, "I don't take little cases like yours, but I feel so sorry for you. I will represent you, but you won't get any money now. I'm just going to see if I could get you a little bit of something to get you through." He agreed to represent me, not making any promises, and I returned home to my studio apartment.

I didn't know what was going to come from that. At that point, hope was just a word. The upside was that I ate and had a possibility. I had a roof over my head for now with a looming eviction. I had no furniture in my place. All I could afford while working was getting to work. I had been sleeping on my floor, and that's where I rested my head for another night.

The next day, I decided to go for a walk. Just like the

day before, a man saw me at my worst. This time, however, it was different. He pulled over in an SUV truck and asked if I was okay because I was crying. I vented to him about my problems. Moving into the apartment, getting in a car accident, and not having any furniture. I was naive and talked to anyone who would listen because I didn't have anyone. The man the day before was nice, and maybe he would be too.

He said, "I have furniture."

I was so tired of sleeping on the floor that I was happy for whatever someone would give me. With no hesitation, I got in the car with him to go see the furniture and bring it back to my apartment. Two hours later, I realized it was all a mistake!

For two weeks, I was forced to engage in sex trafficking and have sex with strangers. He threatened to kill me if I tried to leave. I had no idea where my location was. I was highly monitored and couldn't go out unless forced to perform sex acts. Ironically, I always kept a little pocket Bible in my purse that my great-grandfather had given me. When he abducted me, I had that purse on me and my Bible by my side. I didn't know what sex trafficking was. I just knew that what I was enduring was not right! I wasn't willfully involving myself in anything. I was forced into sex.

One morning I pulled out my Bible, and the abductor's mood shifted. The Bible sparked something on the inside of him that made him angry. He started to speak about how he hated Christians and how God was not going to deliver me from this. He owned me, and I belonged where I was. I didn't know my location, but I knew the length of time I was in his car to get there. Based on that, I could tell I was a two hour ride out, trapped in a house. He had several guns and a twenty-four hour monitoring system so that I couldn't leave.

I would ride in a car and then get out only to be taken into hotels where strangers had sex with me against my will. He would sit out in the front to ensure I couldn't escape. I did what I was told, but I felt like God would deliver me. It was not over for me. I was praying every day, but one particular day, God answered me. I was ordered to have sex with a man in his home. When I entered, he said he was going to go in the shower quickly. I sat there listening to him and noticed that he had an open window. This was my shot at freedom. If I timed this just right, I could get away. I kept my eyes on him and the window. When he stepped out of the room to go to the bathroom, I jumped out of the window.

I never looked back. I ran through miles of woods. All around me were trees and sky. My feet never stopped. I couldn't risk falling or looking back and being caught. I had to stay focused and run until I saw a sign of help somewhere. I was running for what seemed to be forever, and then I reached a street. I couldn't help but cry because ahead of me on that street was a Greyhound station. This was nothing but the grace of God. It was about six o'clock in the morning, and I ran into the Greyhound station. There was an urgency in my spirit to take a bus immediately.

When I checked the schedule there was a bus leaving to return to L.A. at 6:30 a.m. I paused, remembering that I didn't have my ID because when I was taken, all I had was a little bag with two dollars in change and my small pocket Bible. I got to a train crew member, and he was asking for my ID. I panicked. I kept looking over my shoulder because I knew the abductor would be looking for me once he realized I had escaped. I had to tell the truth.

I told him, "I've been abducted into sex trafficking, and I need to get back to L.A. immediately, right away."

I found favor with the crew member, and he blessed me. I had no time to wait for the police to arrive. I needed to escape right away. He allowed me on the 6:30 a.m. bus that was already boarding. I got in a seat and cried the entire ride back.

I questioned everything. Why were these things happening to me? I had no clue who the man was or why he abused me. How could I move to California and lose it all? What was I going to do when I got back? Why did that car accident happen? It was one of the longest rides I ever endured. All I wanted to do was continue school with supportive parents, and I was instead broke and about to be evicted from an apartment. What was my future?

I returned hours later that morning, back to the apartment on Cherokee Avenue. I wanted to go to my apartment in solace, but the first thing I saw was the eviction notice on my door. I ran into the residential manager, David. He questioned where I was because he noticed I was missing around the neighborhood. He hadn't seen me in a while. I told him about my abduction, and I no longer felt safe staying there. I thought he would have some compassion, kind words, or advice for me.

He said, "Listen, you do have to leave this apartment because you can't pay for it. You've already been given an eviction notice, and the sheriff will come and throw your stuff outside eventually."

Another thorn in my side.

With nowhere to go and strapped for cash, I walked to a nearby coffee shop, Solar de Cahuenga, to clear my mind. There, I met a man named Jimmy who was sitting quietly in the corner next to the only empty seat left, having a cappuccino. Although I had been traumatized by the abduction, I wasn't scared to speak to new people. I was put in a place of not having a choice. I just needed better discernment. Jimmy asked me about myself. I shared with him that I was fearful of staying at my place and had escaped sex trafficking. He told me that he owned Castle Ivar in Hollywood. Jimmy offered me a place to stay. He opened his home and allowed me to stay a few days at the very top of his castle, which had a guest room.

I started to see how God kept coming in when I was at my lowest to pull me out. God works in mysterious ways and did so myriad times in my life. My capacity to understand God wasn't developed yet, but I knew He heard my prayers and would continue to send provision, even if money never touched my hands.

The time with Jimmy was nice and helped me when I needed it. I was planning my next move, and then my phone rang. I randomly got a call from someone from my past named Allen. He came from a wealthy political family planted in Washington, D.C., but he grew up in a mansion in Potomac, Maryland, with plenty of disposable income. We dated when I was in eighth grade and about thirteen years old. We randomly reconnected while he was outside my great-grandparent's house before I officially left for L.A. When we first met, he was about sixteen with a driver who chauffeured him around everywhere he wanted. He went to a fancy private school and never attended a public school.

The first time I saw his home, I thought, *Whoa, I wonder what his family does. Are they politicians?*

They were indeed.

When I answered the call, he told me he was in California. I knew he was coming because one of my best friends spilled the beans weeks prior. He told me Allen was coming but told me I was not to say how I knew. When I thought of Allen and his life, I didn't want to let him know what was happening to me. I was embarrassed and broke. I had nothing to show for living in L.A. except for horror stories. I didn't want to be judged by him because he was a wealthy, spoiled, rich kid. He asked if we could meet later that night, and I agreed. I didn't have anything to lose.

CHAPTER 2

Navigating the Storm

MUDDY PUDDLES AREN'T CLEAN.

– Chantel Dean

When Allen came to pick me up, he was driving a very nice BMW. It felt good to be in a car going somewhere nice. He drove me to his place, which was a three-bedroom house in Glendale, California. It was a fully furnished home. As I walked around and saw how beautiful his home was, I pictured where I would be sleeping that night. He had a cozy starter home with an orange tree in the back and a garage separate from the house. The artwork, the beautiful couches. He had all of that square footage for himself, and I had zilch. I lost my composure and succumbed to tears. He wanted to know what was going on, but I couldn't tell him the whole story. How would he react? I kept most of it to myself and only told him that I didn't have anywhere to go and that I was getting evicted from my apartment.

What I believe to have been God's divine intervention happened in the next moment.

He asked me, "Why don't you get all your stuff and move in with me tonight?"

I looked at him. Could this be? Me, living there?

Before I said something I would regret, I told him, "I don't have much of anything and certainly not as much as you, truth is, I came to California with just a suitcase."

That's all I had in that studio apartment on Cherokee. None of that mattered to him. We hopped in the car, and he drove me back. I picked up my bag and moved into his home. I couldn't believe it. I went from being evicted to living with a wealthy kid I randomly dated in eighth grade.

Life started to look up for me. Whatever I wanted, I received. Allen didn't mind doing things for me. I wanted a puppy, and Allen ordered me a puppy online. He could buy anything. He could do anything.

We went to the grocery store and shopping, and all I could say was, "My God, I am blessed." I no longer worried about where my next meal would come from. I had multiple rooms and beds to choose from. All those nights of starvation were over. I was in such a better place. Being with Allen seemed to be a dream come true. I was where I wanted to live and able to finally explore L.A. without limits.

One day, things started to change. When we were younger, I saw Allen's tendencies to mishandle people. He cursed his driver out and became rude as a teenager. I remembered telling my grandmother I was not sure about him because he was spoiled, and that's just not how I was raised. Those red flags were waving in our newfound relationship. He slowly began to degrade me. Not long after the emotional abuse, the physical abuse emerged. I was trapped once again, but this time by someone I thought cared about me. I found myself in an abusive relationship at age eighteen.

The abuse started pretty quickly after I moved in with him. He was sweet to get me in his home because he knew I was vulnerable, but then he became controlling.

One night he told me, "I could kill you, and no one would care."

The car accident didn't kill me, but I was sure Allen would. The same food that was freely given originally was now tied to control. I could no longer open the refrigerator without asking him for permission.

Oftentimes, I was reminded of how much he contributed. He would constantly monitor my phone calls to make sure I wasn't telling people about the abuse. I didn't. I lived everyday in the fantasy world of Allen's mind. I dealt with his behavior for months, still praying and asking God why. What did I do so wrong? Why did bad people find me?

Being in an abusive relationship was something I never thought I would experience. At a young age, I had to move in with my great-grandparents and grandmother because my mom had been through domestic violence. I had grown up in a household where it was prevalent and didn't want to ever go back. It happened so fast that I didn't even understand at that young age what abuse was. Now, being older, I saw first hand what it was. I was eighteen living with this very handsome guy whose family was wealthy and well-known, but he was abusing me. First, it started with emotional abuse making me feel worthless and devalued. Then, he began to slam things and punch the walls before he moved on to hitting me. He would accuse me of cheating when I walked to the corner store, saying that I was going out to meet with my boyfriend— anything to get himself angry enough to cause a physical fight. Then it would become a very abusive situation.

I began praying, "God, if you ever get me out of this..."

Many people talk about domestic violence and why victims don't leave. A lot of times, people cannot afford to exit. Where would I have gone? Many stay because the abuser is also the provider, and they have no other support. I would have been homeless and starving if I had left. I was one of those women who stayed because I didn't have the resources to go. I had no family in L.A. and an eviction under my belt. I had no money or job. I had no opportunity to make friends, and Allen hated the ones I had met.

The only saving grace I had was the accident. There was hope that maybe I would receive a payment and be able to take care of myself. Every couple of months, faithfully, I would go back to the law office and check in. It was always the same thing.

I would meet in person only to hear, "No, I don't think we'll be able to help you because you didn't have insurance. A law was passed. If you don't have insurance, you can't get any money."

Defeated, I would return back to the house. I depended on him for food and to drive me places. I relied on him for everything, and I had no way to escape this abusive situation. After months of the abuse, I wanted to leave. I cried out to God and told Him I wanted to kill myself, believing it was my only way out. I tried to commit suicide by taking a handful of pills. Allen saw me and called the police. Minutes later, officers came and I was taken to Glendale Memorial Hospital, where I was placed under a 5150. A 5150 is a section of the California Welfare and Institutions Code that allows for the involuntary detention of an adult experiencing a mental health crisis. As I came back to myself, I picked up the phone to call Allen to come and get me. I called to no avail. He never answered. There I was again, alone with no one to call.

I stayed as long as they allowed me to, but my release date came. Since Allen never called back, I had to walk back to the house. He was gone entirely when I returned. Eventually we spoke, and he told me that he went back to Potomac, Maryland. He allowed me to continue to live in the home without him. I had unspeakable joy. I thanked God. He made a way for me to get out of an abusive relationship. He removed Allen from me. I don't want to glorify suicide, but the act of it made him realize how much he was destroying me as a person. He just got up and left. No note, no call, no show. He was gone, and he took the car.

My happiness was fleeting. I found myself sad and depressed. I surprisingly was missing my abuser, but how? Why would he just leave me like that? I was hurt because I loved him. He was all I had and all I knew. He provided for me so that I wouldn't have to live on the street, but also beat me down for it. I was on a rollercoaster of emotions, but this was my blessing in disguise. I no longer wanted to die, I wanted to live. I was in a gorgeous, furnished house in Glendale, California. Although I didn't have a car, I could walk around to different places because it was in a good location. I could get a job and have a place to lay my head. I had food. I had all that I needed and my puppy to share it with.

Just when I thought, *God, I'm in such a great place*, He showed me there was more. Just when I thought there was no one, a destiny helper showed up. A college friend introduced me to art modeling, and that was my next job. I was posing for many artists at the Los Angeles Academy of Figurative Art and made $20 an hour. I had a home and my own income to purchase what I wanted and needed. This was my first real artistic job in California, but I still didn't have a car. The bus system had favored me and was my only source of transportation. From my mishap before with the dishwasher position, I learned the schedule because it took many different buses to get there. Unlike the last job, I enjoyed this one. It made taking the different buses worth it.

I was beginning to appreciate where I was and thankful that I had arrived in this place in my life of ease. All the while, I was still going through the car accident case. A blissful couple of months later, I was on my feet. California did not have me sucked into a hole like the first few months. I was thriving. My phone rang and it was a call from the law office. I was doing so well by then, the case was in the back of my mind. To my surprise, it was J. Shaffer.

He said, "You need to come into the office right away."

I thought, *I forgot all about this. He already told me he can't do anything for me, so maybe it'll be a couple hundred dollars or something. Whatever it is, it will help me out.*

Not wanting to procrastinate, I took the bus to Beverly Hills from Glendale. I walked into the building just as I had done before. I sat down outside of where his office was for a few moments, and I saw Mildred passing by doing her work. We spoke to one another with simple small talk. I once again entered into J. Shaffer's personal office. I stepped only a foot in, and I saw his face was lit up. He seemed so happy as I went to take a seat.

No sooner had I done so than he said, "You must have an angel! You've got something miraculous about your life because, remember, I told you I couldn't get you any money."

I nodded in agreement, wondering what he was going to say.

"A law was passed because you didn't have insurance. You couldn't get a settlement. The only thing that overrides that is a drunk driver. Because the woman who hit you—out of all the people that could have hit you—was a drunk driver, your case just settled for $60,000."

The way I hollered. I couldn't believe it. My God, how He works! I could have been hit by dozens of different drivers that night, but because the person who collided with me was drunk, I was given a hefty settlement. This was such an unexpected miracle. I thanked J. Shaffer for even taking me on and working to help me. After signing some paperwork, he put the check in my hands. After all of the pain and suffering I endured from that car accident, I left his office with a $30,000 check that day. That was the remainder after the lawyer's fee.

I started to think about what to do with the money. I immediately went to Bank of the West to cash the check. That $30,000 was the most money I ever had. With that much in my pocket, I was not taking the bus back home. I finally had money and got a taxi. This was before the days of Uber and Lyft services. The way I felt not having to take four to five buses to get home or walk miles to the bus stop was uplifting. My legs and feet could finally rest, and I could get back at a reasonable time.

As I approached the house, I saw a "For Sale" sign on a three-series BMW car in my neighborhood.

I knocked on the door of a brick house with a small driveway and said, "I want to buy your car today."

An older woman replied, "It's $12,000." Given I looked so young, she stared at me and asked, "How are you going to buy that?"

I told her, "I have $12,000 cash right now, and I can get it today."

She allowed me in her home and took me to her living room. I sat down on her couch and counted the cash in front of her. We exchanged money for keys on the spot. Out of the blue, I went from having no car to having one and from being broke to having $18,000 after purchasing the car. Life was good.

The problem was, I had no financial literacy, no training, or advice on how to spend money. I was still under twenty-one years old. I blew the money. I purchased the car and then went on shopping sprees at the Beverly Center. It didn't take long before the money dwindled down to almost nothing. I didn't create a savings account to prepare for a rainy day—and that day came a few months later. I received a call from Allen saying he was returning to get the rest of his belongings. I waited for him, but he never showed up. He called again and told me to send his items to Potomac, Maryland.

Shortly after receiving what he asked for, he put me out of the house. It was like his presence in my life shifted all that I had acquired. My peace, happiness, income, everything. I was finally in such a great place, and he showed up to ruin it. It was this thing inside of him that found joy in my suffering. He loved to see me panic and cry. Even though he was in Maryland, he was still controlling my emotional reactions. I felt I should have been grateful because he let me stay in the home for so long and provided material things that I needed. The issue was none of the things he gave me was worth the pain that I endured. What was I going to do? I spent all my money and never thought to use that last $18,000 to get my own place while continuing to model. I was young and immature. I loaded all I had in my car which included my dog. It was the last thing that bonded us. Allen and I came up with his name, Danger. It was one of the first things he bought for me that I really wanted. I left that day and once again was homeless. Allen didn't care.

Since I had a car, it became my home. I slept in it for three months in L.A., anywhere that I could find—garages, open parking spaces, parks—you name it. The longest place that I slept was a parking lot near Warner Brothers Studios. To care for Danger, I would park my car in parking structures to keep it out of the sun.

Just as I thought I couldn't get any lower, God sent another angel in human form. He came out of nowhere, and gave me a key card to the Oakwood Apartments.

This was a gated community with a shower, theater, and computer room. All paying tenants were allotted these amenities with the use of their key card. Being homeless, this was crucial for me because it allowed me to sleep in my car and have a place to shower every day and get ready. It also had a pool and other nice conveniences. It was as if I lived there.

I was cautious about my moves. A few people noticed me and knew I was homeless, but I took such great care of myself and didn't bother anyone that they didn't mind me using their services. In a split second, all of that changed. I was caught. One of the people who knew I was homeless saw me entering the gate.

Another guardian angel came up to me and said, "They found out you're using our facilities. I'll give you another key card for a building around the corner."

I was in awe. I didn't have time to sit in sorrow. God had already made a way out for me. This wasn't the same person who gave me a key card the first time. God was always working, even when things seemed to be falling apart.

I was thankful and took the key card, but I knew that I had to be even more discreet this time around. Sometimes I would drive up into the hills of Glendale, where there were lovely homes and parks, and sleep there to see the sunrise when I woke up. I would sit and get some inspiration and a word from God. I parked on residential streets in Beverly Hills to sleep and carried around a blanket in my trunk that I used to cover myself on cold nights so that I didn't have to run my gas. Glendale was where I often spent my time because I knew that area.

I frequented the Brand Park Library to read and grow in knowledge since I never gained the conventional college experience. Exercising was important to me too, so I hiked the trails. I was used to walking a lot and wanted to keep up my stamina for possible roles that I could get or jobs that may need me. When you're homeless, it becomes difficult to take care of the day-to-day necessities quickly. I was gaining life experience going through these different storms, although I didn't know it yet.

In all of this, I was trying to figure out where I would live because three months went by so fast. Living out of a car and the paranoia of getting caught showering in an apartment complex where I didn't live was getting to me. I could no longer keep driving to the Los Angeles Academy of Figurative Art in Van Nuys for the art modeling job. Although I loved the work, it was too far away, even with a car. The money I made went straight to the gas tank getting me to and from, and food to eat. I had to eat fast food, and that cost began to add up quickly. I started looking for jobs and applied for a hostess position at Katsuya in the Glendale

Americana. I was relieved when they hired me. Katsuya, an innovative Japanese restaurant and celebrity hotspot blocks from the home I once shared with Allen.

I worked any shift available so that I could make as much money as possible to get out of my car. I had a job near where I wanted to live and a car to get me to and from work. All I needed was a place to live. Craigslist was the major place to find anything. I knew if I was going to find a home, it would be listed there. I found two guys who wanted a roommate, and I reached out to them a few weeks later. I knew what they were asking for in rent, and I didn't have it yet. So I started saving my pay. As long as no one else offered them more than me or was able to pay them before I could, the room would be mine. After three months of homelessness, sleeping in my car with a dog, I saved $2,500 and could rent a room at 1521 W. Glenoaks Blvd. I shared that space with two roomates named Matt & Tim.

The day I moved in was a sour one for me. It seemed that my life had a balance. For all the good I received, bad was always waiting for me on the other end. I had accumulated several parking tickets while living in my car that I never paid. So the day I moved into the room, I heard an alarm going off. It had been over ten minutes, and I wondered why someone wouldn't shut it off. I went outside to discover what was happening only to see the car was mine. The car that I owned outright was being taken away because of all the tickets that I had gotten. It was my fault, but why at this time? I had to park in all those different places. I was homeless and just tried to find a spot to sleep. Why that day? I finally had a place to live. Why couldn't I have it all?

There was no reason to fight it. The authorities were right. I didn't pay the tickets, and they were justified in taking the car. I moved into my room and just laid there thinking. It was the grace of God that the car didn't get taken any other time because that had been my home for three months. They could have taken it while I was at work before I got this place. Getting the car back was not something that I was capable of at that time. I would have to pay for the tickets and the tow. I spent the last of my money on a roof to go over my head. So, there I was again. No longer homeless, but no longer having a car for transportation.

I walked every day from GlenOaks and Sonora to the Americana, which was about a sixty minute walk in the sweltering heat of the California sun. I wasn't making enough money to get my car back or cover anything else besides my rent, so I took a second job at Subway in the mornings. Even with two jobs, the pay was still insufficient. I saved money because I walked everywhere. Around 5 a.m., I would stride to the Subway in Burbank to open by 7 a.m., and then hostess in the evenings. I knew it was time for a change and commenced searching for a church in my area and people who could pray for me. I needed more, and the only person I knew who could help me was God. I was stuck in this place, and although I was grateful, there had to be more for me. I discovered Glendale Church of God with Pastor Sean and Sister Lashay while living at GlenOaks and Sonora. I would walk about seven miles to church on Sunday mornings because trying to maintain that relationship with God was so important to keep my sanity. Although I wasn't always consistent, I tried to maintain my relationship with God as much as I possibly could. For one year, that became my routine.

Time passed, and I still needed to make more money. The two jobs were not enough. I needed to be a server because they made cash in tips every day. Not only would I have a check at the end of the week, but I would have money every day for my financial needs. I was so busy, I didn't have time to look around for a job. God led me to where I needed to be. Hungry, I walked into a restaurant in Glendale called Gauchos Village. It was a Brazilian steakhouse owned by a Brazilian man named Kevin. My shoes were torn and flapping from walking everywhere. Unaware of the identity of the person I was speaking to, I didn't have the energy to give my story.

All I said was, "I'm starving."

Kevin let me into his restaurant and allowed me to

make a plate from the buffet-style Brazilian steakhouse similar to a Fogo de Chao.

"It's on the house, so don't worry about it," he said before asking, "Would you like to work here?"

I asked, "Do you need a server? I'm already a hostess at another restaurant, but I want the ability to receive tips."

He said yes and to come back at five o'clock with different shoes. I was so excited but the downside was that I didn't have any other shoes. As a result of my finances, there was no money to get new shoes. I returned with the same shoes on. Kevin looked down at my feet, then up at my face. He perceived without saying anything that was all I had. He gave me money to go to the Americana to buy new work shoes. From that day forward, I worked at Gaucho's Village and became a part of his family-owned business. He treated me like his family and even allowed me to come to his house for dinner.

Things were beginning to look up for me. Kevin saw a problem and helped me with no ulterior motives. I finally found a support system with him and his family. I had a community that looked out for me. I didn't have all the things I wanted, but I was on the path to getting there. What could possibly go wrong?

CHAPTER 3

Unexpected Downpours

WHEN IT RAINS, IT POURS.
– Chantel Dean

Working at Gauchos Village was such an answered prayer. Leaving for the day with money in my pocket to do simple things was a feeling beyond words for me. Meeting new people was a part of the job, but eventually, I started to recognize the regular customers who frequented the restaurant weekly or daily. As I worked with many people, I got close to a few coworkers. Two were a set of caucasian twins named Kori and Kody. We would go to Tommy's Burgers in Glendale together after work near their apartment with their female roommate named Marocel. We laughed and talked about the work day as we walked to the restaurant. Once we sat down inside, we discussed over burgers and chili fries everything we had been through. When topics were hard to bear, she knew how to comfort me when I was entering certain emotional spaces.

Marocel worked at Gauchos Village as a bartender when I started as a server. She was about ten years older than me, and I looked up to her like a big sister. She was a beautiful Filipino girl from Florida with gorgeous tan skin. Her hair was long and flowing, reaching down her back. Being around her was exactly what I needed given feminine comradery was missing in my life. I was eager to learn everything she knew, and she didn't mind teaching me. She educated me a lot about her culture, how to cook certain dishes, and how to form a friendship. When I needed it the most, she allowed me a shoulder to cry on about Allen.

Her timing in my life could not have been any more perfect, considering I was growing further apart from people in my hometown and losing the closeness I once had with my best girl friends. My trips back to D.C. were becoming less frequent as I was growing into adulthood and spending more on bills and less on travel. People move, grow apart, lose and build new relationships with others. After a while, people lose touch with themselves, making them lose touch with others. Marocel gave me a friendship you don't often find in the big city. In places like Los Angeles, people come and go, so you feel like you don't have anyone. It was tough to build connections to others, so I held on when I found someone who could be a good girlfriend.

There was one occasion where Marocel hosted a Thanksgiving gathering at their apartment for the twins and me. This was important since our families were far away, and we still wanted to celebrate the holidays. I couldn't thank her enough for acknowledging that, even though we were far from our families, we still had each other. We formed a bond and were two peas in a pod—her and I. Her presence in my life was crucial. She was a true friend and sister. I didn't have much of anything at the time. She noticed my lack of everyday necessities but never criticized me. She was an answer to my problems. Have you ever met someone who seemed to be the solution you needed? She shared clothes with me and welcomed me into the apartment with the twins. I never felt like an outsider when I was in their place. Being there all the time is how I got involved with Kori and Kody. Not only was I at work with them, but I was in their home daily too.

Marocel had a great head on her shoulders and wanted more out of life. She didn't want the drag of Los Angeles living to bring her down and decided to go back to school for nursing. She wasn't going to quit her job as a bartender but dropped her hours down to part-time so that she had the availability to do both. Concerned about my future, she urged me to think about what I wanted to do and where I wanted to go. Yes, things had not gone as planned, and I couldn't be a server forever. That is not what I went to California to do.

I heard everything she was saying but couldn't think about the future when the past haunted me. The only way to get to Marocel's was by passing the Kenwood house where I lived with Allen. It was a reminder of someone constantly belittling me and not caring what happened to me. It was the house of false dreams and lies. It wasn't the memories of him that hurt the most but the people in my life who told me to get over it and move on. That was hard to do, and heartbreak takes time to heal. There's no time limit on grief. It can hit you on a warm sunny day when everything seems okay. In the next minute, you feel wetness on your face and somehow find yourself in tears over the past.

This was why Marocel was so important to me. She gave me room to cry and to be confused. I didn't have to have the answers or know the next steps. She let me tell my story and get it out. She was one of my first therapists in a way because of her understanding of me. She knew what it felt like to be overlooked and surrounded by people who do not have compassion for what you have been through. We took care of each other. For instance, at Tommy's she would cover the few extra dollars I needed and vice versa when there wasn't enough for our meals. We shared secrets that we had never told anyone else. I confided in her about my sex trafficking experience and how I was able to escape. We looked at fancy cars we knew we couldn't afford and pictured ourselves driving them one day. We even browsed for wedding dresses together in Glendale. I had a best friend, a sister, and a confidant, all wrapped in one.

To gain someone and lose them so quickly makes my stomach knot up thinking about it. Everything happened so fast. Marocel and I were living life as best friends for more than a year, and then she met a man named Rich. She told me she was leaving for the weekend to go to Catalina Island for a date with him. It must have been one hell of a date because right after, she told me she was moving to Texas with him on the following Monday. I was devastated. Who was Rich? She was in school and working. How could she give all of that up for some man she just met? What happened in Catalina? It wasn't any of my business, but this pattern of loss was becoming my California life. As soon as I thought I had it all figured out—bam! Another slap in the face. How could he just take my best friend? My thoughts raced as I helped her pack. I didn't want to bring her down, so I kept my feelings bottled up.

In true Marocel style, she gave me most of her things. She didn't have room to pack them and knew that I could use them. We went to Tommy's for the last time and cried. I couldn't even eat my food because I knew things would change after that moment. I was happy for her to get out of the struggles of California but sad at the same time because she was the only one in my corner. I walked past 132 South Kenwood to GlenOaks and Sonora. I wept the entire walk home about everything. Where was my life going? The one good friend I had was leaving. I felt like being with her was a home away from home. Who would I be with? Not only did we work together, but we broke bread together. I wondered, *Why do bad things keep happening to me?* I no longer wanted to live. I only had two choices: take my life or get help. I walked in my apartment and called the suicide hotline.

One of the two roommates I had at the time was named Tim. We barely saw each other because I was either at work or with Marocel. He overheard me on the phone and knocked on my door, but I didn't answer. I was caught up in what I was going through. It was too painful to process another person leaving me. Feelings of abandonment rose up within me stemming from my dad leaving, Allen, and now Marocel. Everyone around me abandoned me. I sat on that phone and cried as they pulled me off the edge. I fell asleep on my bed worn out with no tears left to spare.

The following day, Tim returned to my door. This time, I opened it for him. He wanted to make sure I was okay and asked if I wanted to go on set with him to work on a series he was doing with Panic! At the Disco, a pop rock band. Of course I did! I was very familiar with them from my high school years from getting ready for school to their music on MTV jams. They were filming a series called *Good Cops* and needed an extra actress for the scene. I pulled myself together and went on set with Tim. I was able to get an IMDb page because of that day. I began to feel like a real actress because they treated me like one. I was able to ride with the band, and afterward, they dropped me off at home. I needed that to uplift my spirit.

Tim took me on the set when I was so depressed, feeling suicidal, and worthless. He was just being a good person, but his kindness changed my outlook on life. He lit a fire back in me. He reminded me that I had come to Los Angeles to be a star, and all I'd been doing was working in restaurants. At a certain point, I just stopped going to auditions and acting classes. I stopped trying. My dreams started to feel impossible with the way my life was going. I gave up everything because I needed money, but God had continued to make a way for me to survive. Tim's deed might have seemed so small for him, but it was huge for me. I continued to work without my friend and life didn't seem so bad after being on set. I was ready to get back to my love of acting and filming.

The only people I had were Kori and Kody. One day Kody said, "I'm going to move back to Missouri. Los Angeles is not my thing."

His statement didn't concern me until Kori invited me to be his roommate. The only catch was he would be moving to another apartment. The new place would be on Burton Way. I needed something different, and I was tired of living in that GlenOaks and Sonora room. It was loud and noisy there, and I wanted to move. I knew I needed to move, and I had to make a choice. I decided to become Kori's new roommate.

Danger and I settled into an apartment at 8722 Burton Way in the heart of Los Angeles. We were two blocks from the Four Seasons Hotel on Doheny Drive, so it got me thinking. Not only did I have a new place, but I needed a new job. Instead of taking two buses to Glendale and going to Gauchos Village, I could get a job at Four Seasons. I had to get up so much earlier just to make it to work on time. I walked around the corner and asked if they were hiring. Security staff on duty mentioned there was just one position in room service.

Immediately I said, "I want to take it," and I was hired. Just like that, I got a job at the Four Seasons in Beverly Hills.

Living with Kori was not what I expected. I was used to the banter of the twins and Marocel. With just the two of us, laughter and joy was absent. Shortly after setting up our things, Kori moved his boyfriend in, and they fought constantly. It had become the norm after a long day of work to come home to arguing. As I lay on my bed trying to get some rest, I heard something and couldn't believe it. Kori had an opioid addiction. The guy he was dating was a doctor, and Kori was fighting with him, saying he wanted to get more opioid pills. I didn't want to get involved, but the yelling went on for more than an hour. A pillow over my head didn't work, nothing. I finally got out of bed and walked up the hallway. I was training for my new job at the Four Seasons and had to be there at 6 a.m.

Exhausted, I pleaded, "Please, I have to get up early in the morning."

I needed to go to sleep. At that moment, for no reason at all, Kori looked at me and said, "I don't care what you have to do, nigger."

I didn't retaliate. I was stunned that he would say that. I had been around him and never once did he seem like the type of person to say something like that to me. There wasn't any time to react because there was a loud knock at the door. It was the police. One of the neighbors called the cops on them because the fighting was so loud.

I had already paid Kori half the rent on the first day, and this was the day after. While the police were in the room, I called a friend. He was a nice caucasian man named Todd who I had randomly met at Gauchos Village while I was there working.

He seemed to be an okay person and had told me, "If you ever need anything, call me."

I smiled and took his number, thinking that I would never need it. When I dialed him up, I first had to remind him who I was.

"Hi, I'm the waitress you met at Gauchos Village. You told me to call you if I ever needed something."

He let me know that he knew exactly who I was.

I sighed in relief and continued, "I'm working at the Four Seasons, but I have a problem. My roommate just called me a nigger, and I'm not staying at this house anymore."

Not even fifteen minutes later, a black stretch limo was outside the apartment. It was Todd in the limo that he owned. I greeted him and let him know I would be right out. While Kori and his boyfriend were in the room with the police from their fight, I was making moves. I packed up the little bit that I had along with my dog into Todd's limo. That night, I moved in with

Todd to 350 S. Cloverdale Ave in Miracle Mile. That word "Miracle" just kept ringing bells in my life. As I walked into Todd's home, the feeling of sadness crept over me. Someone that I used to call a friend so freely had openly called me a nigger. Confusion laid within me because Kori had invited me to his church but had so much hate in his heart. How could that be? I recognized that racist people will tolerate you, but they will not like you. It was hard to grasp because that was the first time I was ever called nigger to my face.

After getting inside of Todd's place that night, I cried. I poured out everything I felt on his couch. There were so many different reasons that I was hurting. I knew racism was still around, but I didn't know it would meet me in that way. I paid my hard-earned money to live there but was transported to someone's couch. I was homeless again. I wasn't in a car or on the street, but I wasn't in a place of my own. Todd gave me whatever linens were available and told me that I could stay there. I told him the whole story and he agreed that Burton Way was not where I needed to be.

Looking back at Kori, the only scripture I can think of is Psalm 110:1: "Sit at my right hand until I make your enemies a footstool for your feet." God showed me He would do it and taught me a lesson. I learned about having the gift of discernment and using it with people.

Actions do speak louder than words, and people can change based on who they are around. Some will not like you because of the color of your skin, and that's their problem not yours. I didn't do anything wrong to be called out of my name. I remember the story of how my great-grandfather was the first African-American sergeant in the military over an all-white platoon because he was the only one who could read and write.

A racist soldier couldn't handle being in the military. He went to my grandfather and said, "I want to go home, nigger," and pointed a pistol at my grandfather to kill him.

My grandfather put his thumb on the barrel, and the soldier pulled the trigger. It blew off my grandfather's thumb. He still served as the top sergeant despite his fellow soilders attempt on his life. He didn't let that stop him and I wasnt going to let my situation stop me.

Although displaced, I woke up the next day strategizing my next move. I met another new girlfriend that day, a unique Black woman named Eboni. She was a Los Angeles native, and her mother was a former member of the Black Panther Party in Oakland, California. My relationship with Eboni was extraordinary. She lived across the street from Todd and would come over often because he would have small cookouts on the front porch on Sundays. Meeting her for the first time was just an experience. She was always pro-Black and the sister I needed.

Eboni was in medical school at UCLA to become an OBGYN. She was a fantastic human being and taught me everything about Miracle Mile. She also didn't own a vehicle, so we walked everywhere. My walks were different sharing them with her. She would take the bus to UCLA daily, which I admired. She always told me stories about when her mom was a Black Panther and how I had to stand up for myself as a Black woman. I loved her because she taught me how to speak up for myself, stand up for myself, and love myself in a way that we're not always taught as Black people.

She gave me several books to read and said, "You're going to learn while I'm learning, and you're going to be great. It doesn't matter what you've been through because you have so much purpose in your life."

She spoke life over me because she knew I was depressed from sleeping on someone else's couch.

I appreciated her, but I was questioning my life. I had no idea what I was doing from day to day. I felt very lost. It was like I was moving to Los Angeles for the first time again. I considered telling my great-grandparents what was happening, but why worry them? I did have a roof over my head and a job. It wasn't that bad, but I needed a new focus, and I found that in Eboni. She became my mentor. I started to see myself in her because she was a woman who looked like me and was doing great things. Having the ability to be honest and open with her was my biggest game-changer. She provided a warm shoulder for my tears, and she truly cared about me.

I was so favored to have that kind of woman in California, even briefly. There were times where she let me know, "I'm not judging you because you don't have the money. I don't care if you don't have it. You're still my friend whether you are on the bus or if your nice car gets taken from tickets and you never get it back."

We both shared a laugh. Laughter got me through those dark days.

"I'll be your friend if you don't have anything at all."

Even with the presence of Eboni, Kori was still around. Thinking back, I always felt frustrated because Kori created anger in me that I didn't deal with until later on in my life. I took the high road. I wanted to retaliate, but I'm glad that I didn't. When I removed myself from the home, I thought everything would be over with Kori, but it wasn't. It's almost like he was mad that I didn't retaliate, and so he began to torment me. For months, Kori continued to harass me with racism. I never returned to his place, so he came to my job at the Four Seasons and dropped off a hate-filled letter for a valet to give to me. I was surprised that he wouldn't let it go. Although I was upset, I ignored him. I trashed the letter. When that didn't work, he took me to court for $10,000. His reasoning was that I defaulted on my lease, but I never signed one with him. He was lying.

It was by the grace of God my credit was so poor that I wasn't under contract with Kori. This was just another example of God's protection in my life, even though I didn't know it at that time. It seemed to him that calling me a nigger wasn't good enough. He needed me to feel his hate. He wanted me to act out and lash back at him. My half of the rent was paid, and I didn't stay there. I was the one who lost my place and ended up on Todd's couch. I removed myself and still dealt with his issues.

After facing all these different storms, I wondered where my life was going. I continued to work at the Four Seasons and lived with Todd. It was a small apartment, but I was able to create a room using a curtain in Todd's dining room. I purchased an air mattress for my bed and set it up. Todd was loving and built a bond with Danger. He helped with walking him when I had early morning or late shifts at The Four Seasons.

I served two years at the Four Seasons and had incredible moments with incredible people. When I was there, all my problems disappeared. I was grateful to meet stars and people who inspired me for years. Even if I was just bringing breakfast, lunch, or dinner to their room, it was an honor. I was living the scripture from Proverbs 18:16: "A man's gifts open doors for him and bring him before great men." I was in front of people I would have never met if it wasn't for the events that took place in my life.

Once Eboni reached her senior year, she became swamped. Our time together was limited, but she had poured so much into me. I used what she put on the inside of me to build up my self-confidence. I could stand on my own two feet again. My inner strength grew. She was like a black panther. Her essence and the sound of her voice were what I needed at that specific time. She challenged me to think further and move out of stagnation. I became a better person and started to believe that my situation didn't make me. It was just a stop on my journey. I was blessed to have a friend like that. I always considered everything a blessing, even Kori. The apartment we had brought me into the city and a chance at a new career. His fighting gave me a reason to contact Todd and have a safe space to live, which brought me to Eboni. I started becoming the Chantel that I always knew I could be.

CHAPTER 4

Misty Rain

THE DRIP DROPS OF LIFE CREATE ITS RHYTHM.

— Chantel Dean

While Eboni was doing all these things to improve my life, I was still in a dark period for many reasons. One of them was that I had no car. Los Angeles is so expensive, and it kept me walking in order to have funds for the bare necessities. Walking everywhere with Eboni was fun and exciting, but alone it was tiring. I walked home after a long day of work and just wanted to lay down, but Todd had this big grin on his face. I couldn't figure out why or what Todd was doing, and there it was. A brand new bike. I couldn't believe it. Todd gifted me a bike. It was just what I needed to raise my spirits. I took it for a test run, and then I rode that bike every day. No matter how hot it was, you could find me down the street on my new wheels. The sun was always out in Los Angeles, and it tried to beat me down with its rays. But the breeze of the wind and the freedom of letting the bike flow down hills was enough for me. I didn't have to walk. The bike seemed to glide down hills, and my feet rested. I would bike from Miracle Mile to Beverly Hills, back and forth to work. My life had gotten easier with Todd, and before I knew it, two years had flown by.

As I adjusted to how my life was going, I got a phone call from the person I would least expect to reach out. It was Allen. It had been years since I had heard from him. His last comments were for me to leave his home, and I was on the street. I hesitated to pick it up, but what could he possibly say? He couldn't do any worse to me than he already had. He reached out to say he was so sorry for everything. Everything. It was the apology I had been waiting years to hear. At that moment I thought, *Wow, he finally understands the way he treated me. He is owning up to abusing me.* It was the closure that I needed from him. Then the conversation took a turn. He told me he was coming back to Los Angeles, and he would love to reconnect with me. Seriously? What did he take me for, a fool? This man hurt me worse than anyone had ever done. He abused me and left me homeless. How dare he want to reconnect with me. For what? To break me down again? I listened and hung up the phone.

I thought that would be the end of Allen, but then my phone was always buzzing because he started sending me love-bombing phone calls. He also sent text messages that were full of "I love you" and "I miss you." I knew he didn't, but I still waffled. I'd gone through sleeping in my car, living on GlenOaks and Sonora, and moving in with a racist roommate. I was living in Todd's apartment. I missed having a bed and the comfort of knowing that everything would be taken care of so much that for a second, I forgot the abuse and said yes to Allen.

Thankfully, it didn't take long before I had a profound revelation. As the words passed between my teeth, I started questioning myself. Was I really that desperate? Going to Allen was material gain, but what I would have to suffer would be greater than anything his money could buy. I immediately called him back.

"Allen, I can't be your friend," I said, feeling as though I was screaming those words at him. I wanted to be his friend, but I knew where that landed me before.

I cried myself to sleep that night. It was the hardest night since I had moved in with Todd. I could have reconnected with Allen. Sitting across from the table, would I have been able to turn him down? I still cared about Allen because he wasn't all bad, but I tried to hurt myself to get out of the relationship years before. It was toxic. What would I even reconnect with him for? To tell him how I was on the street so he could laugh at my misfortune since he left me? It had taken me so much time to work on rebuilding my self-esteem, worth, and healing. So much had happened!

I sat back and looked at myself and realized I was fully healed enough to not say anything more to Allen. It was officially over, and I was okay with that. There was nothing more that I needed from him, not even an explanation because there was nothing he could do or say that would change a thing for me. He couldn't give me back the years or the time I spent on the street and in bad company. I officially let go.

As I laid there on Todd's couch, I knew it was time to get to my own place. Todd had a great heart, but our situation became incredibly hard. It was Kori number two, just not racist. Todd was also a heavy drug user with a closeted cocaine addiction. You can't live with someone for a long time and not get to know them and their secrets. We shared the whole apartment except for our sleeping areas. I saw him using one time when he didn't think that I could see him. After a while, he was comfortable just doing it out in the open. That wasn't the only problem. He was also an alcoholic and could sometimes be a nasty drunk. He would come in from a night out and reek of alcohol. Todd would drink a little too much, a little bit more than usual, and his behavior would become sporadic. In his 50s and frustrated with his life, he coped by relying heavily on drugs and alcohol. I started searching for places to live because his addictions were taking center stage in our home. He became a bit unbearable, loud, and unruly. I was trying to sleep, and he would come in at all times of the night.

The many issues he was dealing with began to show themselves in our tiny space. When I moved in, he only asked me for $500 on the first of every month to sleep on his couch. It was reasonable because I had all that I needed and a place to lay my head. I could afford it and still get the things that I needed. I'd happily hand him $500. I knew he used drugs but not that he was an addict until the money started getting funny. It would be blown within hours. He would go to the bar and get wasted. Everyone in the neighborhood thought it was funny but me. They didn't have to live with the town drunk. Todd started to slowly just crash into depression and drug use.

I still had Eboni to lean on even with her busy schedule until she eventually moved to Leimert Park. I began to feel alone again. I had no one. I thought of people to speak to and my coworker, April, came to mind. She was always nice to me and seemed like a good friend. I contacted her because I desperately needed some fresh air. We hung out. I wasn't looking for anything, but something caught my eye. It was an apartment building with a "For Lease" sign at 8720 West Olympic Boulevard. It was in Beverly Hills. While she was driving, I tapped her on the shoulder and asked her if she could pull over. By pure faith, I got out of the car and used my phone to take a photo of the sign to follow up later. Something just drew me to the building that day. My time with Todd had run out because his closeted addictions were out in the open and began to rear their ugly head. The secret was out, and the real issues began.

I told Eboni that I was looking for a place, and she mentioned moving to the neighborhood of Leimert Park where she was. I thought about it, but it was pretty far without a car from the places that I needed to be. During the day I worked, and at night, I kept looking at that place on Olympic Boulevard. I had to tell Todd. My move was inevitable. As much as I loved the payment and all that he had done for me, it was best that I left. There was no argument, he just nodded in agreement.

He finally let me in a little bit and said, "I do have a problem when I drink."

Todd had been a limo driver for the Rolling Stones along with a host of other celebrities. This was his life for so long, but the transit system began to change. People went from using cabs to getting big limos to travel around and let others know of their celebrity stature. Suddenly, Uber started and began to pick up as the trendy and simpler way to travel. No one wanted to pay for limousines anymore. What was once a symbol of pride and joy for him was becoming just another thing that reminded him of what used to be. He was going through an identity crisis or a midlife crisis.

He had a multitude of friends who were wealthier and more successful than he was, and it bothered him. They had surpassed him. Todd knew my leaving was for the best for our friendship to remain intact. We finally talked, which we had stopped doing. We were in a routine of me coming and going and him being hungover. He suggested that I become a medical receptionist. This was a career that I hadn't thought about before, but it would allow me to leave hospitality and finally have weekends and holidays off to rest. I took his advice and applied for a few medical receptionist positions.

After two years of alternating between an air mattress and Todd's couch, I trusted God for a new place and job. A few weeks after applying, I finally got a call from Khalili Center medical office in Beverly Hills. It was a few blocks from the Four Seasons, where I worked. What I learned is when God is in the room, you will never be denied. I was interviewed by a man who previously worked as a learning manager at the

Four Seasons. He said that although I lacked medical experience, he still hired me because he knew I had five-star service training from the Four Seasons. There God was, making a way out of nowhere. God's strategy was better than anything I could ever do. I was hired because I had worked at a place unrelated to where I was trying to go, simply because the hiring manager had worked there too. With my new job, I was making more money, given better benefits, and had more desirable hours.

I was ready to let Todd know that I was hired because he was the one who guided me to the job. I do believe God put that on Todd's mind to tell me. I told him about the 8720 Olympic Boulevard address, and he knew a guy. Todd was a big-time name-dropper and knew the people he was talking about.

When I mentioned that I was looking at this particular apartment, he said, "My God, my buddy Paul owns that apartment building!"

I can't make these things up. I was in awe. Someone he knew had something I needed. He called Paul who said he would meet me and show me the place that same day. I wasted no time because I didn't want to lose the opportunity. I walked to his office on Doheny, which was about two blocks from the Four Seasons. His leasing office for all of his Beverly Hills properties was there. I walked in knowing that I had no money. I was living paycheck to paycheck. Even without having a lot of bills, I had just enough to be on Todd's couch.

I reached Paul's office ready to give the woe is me, this is all I have speech but didn't have to.

Paul said, "I talked to Todd, and he said that you've been through a lot and a lot is happening in your life. I've never done this before, but I will allow you to move into 8720 Olympic Boulevard apartment six today."

My anxiousness was rising and so was my fear as I heard his words. I could have my own place that day, but how could I afford it?

Then I heard him say to me, "I won't charge the average rent that everyone else is paying, which is $2,500 to live there. I will only charge you $1,200."

Okay, Lord. God had given me this open door, but I started to worry because I didn't have $1,200 to give him that day. I had no idea when I would even get that much money. Then he opened his mouth again. I never had the chance to dwell on the negative because Paul's next words answered my questions.

"I will also let you live there for six months free. I'm going to let you get on your feet and save some money."

What? I couldn't even believe it. Six months free rent. I could save up for the seventh month, get the furniture I wanted, have my own room and bed. Me. I could finally have my own space. Paul handed me a set of keys. The feel of the new keys in my hand was more than I could have dreamed. I walked out of his office with tears in my eyes and called Todd.

"I can move in today," I told him.

I headed over to Olympic Boulevard to see my new place. It was about a six-block walk from Doheny to Olympic and Robertson. I reached the apartment, still unsure if any of this was real. The moment I knew that this was my new life was when I placed the keys in the lock and heard the click. I turned the doorknob and entered my new home. I opened the door and started crying. How was this even happening? God was smiling on me.

Not soon after, I gathered my items from Todd's place and was all moved in. Danger and I once again, had a new home. I knew that I was in major need of home items, and just as before, a financial miracle found me. The Four Seasons called me and said a Dubai Prince who had stayed there left me an $8,000 cash tip for my excellent service. This man blessed me with enough money that I was able to save and get the furniture I needed.

All I could hear were the words spoken so many times in church from the elders in my head, "He may not come when you want, but He's always on time."

I moved into my apartment in the heart of Beverly Hills, where I lived for a few years. My older brother and I were close but I stayed away because of my

California circumstances. I was in a place where I felt proud for my family to see me. My brother came to visit me. He was normally very busy because he was working to become a doctor. With all he had going on , he made time to see me. He checked in as much as he could.

I continued to work but never purchased another car. Living in Los Angeles was expensive enough, even on discounted rent. I was able to get everywhere that I needed. My two feet never failed me. I took pride in walking to the leasing office to pay my rent. It felt fantastic to have the money to pay and not live in fear that I would get evicted. Paul was a very wealthy, humble man. A friendship between us organically formed, and we spent time together. He invited me to parties at his Santa Monica beach house. It was a gorgeous glass home right on the water, worth millions of dollars. I loved going there and taking in the landscape. We not only did social indoor events, he would also take me to baseball games. It was the first time in my life since moving to California that I could enjoy myself. I wasn't pressured or belittled. We enjoyed each other's company, and I was making it on my own, so I wasn't looking for someone to take care of me. It was one of the most lifechanging things for me to have a friend like Paul.

Our relationship led me to a self-reflection journey of people I had come in contact with in my life. Even when they broke me down, they still helped me grow. I was grounded and stable for once, and I questioned my purpose. What I came to L.A. for continued to lead me in a path away from the spotlight. God kept showing up for me when I would hit rock bottom, but I wasn't living the life I saw for myself.

I was beginning to feel a calling on my life. My desire for God was growing, and with that came an urgency to preach. As God picked me up out of these situations, I would share my testimony with others. I spread God's goodness and how He kept me. It was natural for me to speak of God and how what He did for me, He would do for them. A few people told me that I should be preaching. The way I spoke about God, preaching must have been my path. Preaching was a tug of war for me because of my love for the arts. I wanted to be the next break-out star, and that didn't align with preaching. But living in Los Angeles, I was nowhere close to that either. California was sucking the life out of my dreams, and reality was hitting me big time.

I reminisced about the past. Whenever someone told me I sounded like I was preaching to them, I remembered being five years old. Sundays after church I would make my great-grandparents sit on the couch while I ministered to them, just as my great-grandfather did to the congregation. He was a fiery Baptist minister and would end all of his sermons yelling. I wanted to be just like him.

He would say things such as, "He stayed there all day Friday, all Friday night, all day Saturday, all Saturday night, but early, early, early Sunday morning, did he get up?"

He was talking about Jesus, but it was the way he did it.

I admired my great-grandfather, and I grew up closely with him. He pastored for forty years at a small Baptist church in Washington, D.C. just around the corner from our home. I wasn't the typical young girl who was outside with her friends or spent weekends eating cereal and watching cartoons. My Saturdays were spent going with him to nursing homes and prisons. We administered communion and prayed for people. The gift of preaching flowed out of me, and I always told people that I would be a preacher one day. It wasn't a Sunday morning routine for me. I saw it every week and every day! My great-grandfather is the one who gave me my first Bible and set the example of what a father and a man should be. Most girls want to be like a female mentor, but I wanted to be like him. His strength and the power of God that stood in the pulpit with him was astounding. He had an anointing on his life, and I wanted to work for God just like him. If he was Elijah, then call me Elisha.

Sadly, it took years of storms to lead me back to my true calling. The more people reminded me of my true love for God, the more I disconnected from my life in Los Angeles. I felt a strong pull to leave, but I didn't know where to start. I finally had it together, and things were going well for me. However, it was all mediocre. I was living and working a regular job. The only time I lit up was when I was spreading the goodness of God. I bit the bullet and called my great-grandfather with tears in my eyes. I told him that I was ready to accept the call to the pulpit. I would call him through the years in the middle of the night to pray with and for me. I didn't always tell him what was going on, and he didn't ask. Those prayers covered me in times of trouble.

He was not only my father, but also my pastor. I would be tasked with writing my first initial sermon from my desk at the Khalili Center. Although I knew this was my portion, it was hard to write. Preaching was impactful and could build you up or break you down. I had to do this to glorify God and to bring others closer to Him. I titled it, *God Will Turn It Around*. As I went through my Bible, the scriptures about Moses and the children of Israel stood out to me. I created my sermon around Moses leading the Israelites out of Egypt and across the Red Sea on dry land. I was reminded of the miracles bestowed by God. I cried with every pen stroke. I knew I would have to fly back to D.C. and preach this sermon in front of my hometown church to receive my license.

Through the Storm: The Price of Fame

Everything that happened in my life led me there. Every twist and turn since the day I planned to move to California. No matter what I did, my choices led me back to God. The sunny day in May had arrived. It was 2017, and I was boarding a plane. I was leaving the tumultuous California past with my sermon in my hand, ready to share the word of God. I didn't know if my great-grandparents would have room for a dog, so I chose to leave Danger with Todd in California. It was a peaceful flight, and when I landed, I was the bright eyed five-year-old all over again. My great-grandparents were there to meet me at Baltimore/Washington International Airport as proud parents. I was so delighted to see them that I ran up and hugged them. I didn't know how much I missed them until I held them in my arms. I was then ready to be a preacher.

We arrived at their home. I unpacked and prepared for my big day. I stayed in the same home and room I initially grew up in on 13th street in Washington D.C. I attended Sunday school that morning and was taken into my great-grandfather's office to be prayed over by him in the presence of a few other ministers before heading to the pulpit. I was nervous and excited. The time came, and we went into the sanctuary. When they called my name, I went up to the podium to preach. I said the dialogue for my sermon perfectly.

I spoke on God's ability to turn things around in

our lives. I recalled being younger and taking a cruise with my mom and older brother. We did not return to the boat on time and were stranded in Cancun, Mexico. The man at the boat dock told us no boat had turned around in seventeen years. It was through the grace of God and the power of prayer, the ship turned around. An emergency came up with a passenger, and within two minutes of prayer, they had to return. It took three hours before the boat came back, but it did. We were able to walk back on the ship as if it never happened. The congregation enjoyed the sermon, and I was relieved.

I received my license to preach the same day. I was proud of myself for answering the call and to do it in front of my great-grandfather. The trip wasn't long because I had to get back to work, but I wasn't going back to Los Angeles alone. I had God, my license, and the love of my family. I had a lot of time to think on my flight back. Once I returned, my feelings were stronger that I had overstayed my welcome in the city of Lost Angels.

CHAPTER 5

The Living Water

OUR CORE REQUIRES HYDRATION.
— *Chantel Dean*

I RETURNED BACK TO THE HUSTLE AND BUSTLE OF daily life at the medical office. I wasn't ready to go back to my place in Los Angeles because I wanted to work on my purpose. I still had my mind on the bright lights of big-city living, but my heart was in D.C. I stayed for another two years away from home.

Scenarios of what could happen overtook me, and I made swift arrangements to leave. I had no reason to remain in California. Marocel and Eboni, my great friends, had moved. I couldn't count on Todd anymore. I had a normal job, and it was not worth it to continue to be there. I immediately put in my thirty-day notice with Paul. Having my own place was great, but it cost me so much. I told Paul that I was so grateful for all the concessions he made on my behalf, being there for me and understanding the need for me to get on my feet. He was a real friend to me. He took me out and let me see the Los Angeles that everyone was in love with. I appreciated that, but it was no longer enough. Having room and board but no path in life was no longer acceptable for me. I would never burn a bridge, and he understood why I was doing this. He was where he wanted to be and wanted the same for me.

During those last thirty days, I did a lot of inner reflection. I looked at where I was in life and where I wanted to be. Having an inner circle of support was necessary, but I wasn't sure I had a circle. I had missed major celebrations, graduations, and other significant events within my family. I ultimately became detached because I was on the West Coast and they were on the East Coast. When I first moved, people called me and checked on me constantly. It wasn't long before I realized you can get forgotten easily in Los Angeles. It is the out-of-sight, out-of-mind mentality. I can't blame others because I did the same thing. I wasn't keeping in contact with people, and they also fell off on contacting me. My great-grandparents were in their late 90s. I didn't want to add pressure to their life, but I could only imagine them worrying about me, and I was so far away. I realized I had taken my family and church for granted. I turned my back on everyone for the sake of my dreams, which were not coming to fruition.

Right when I thought all that I worked for would be in the trash, I was contacted by my friend Brayden. He went to Baltimore School for the Arts with me and was doing great things in the stage world in New York. He called, and we discussed our lives and how things were going.

He said, "I feel you'd do better in New York than in Los Angeles. You've been there all these years and going through all these different things. You've been struggling. You can't go on like this."

What he said hit me hard because I was in a place where depression would creep on me. I felt that way mainly because I wasn't around my core, my family. They were the people who had known me my whole life and loved me. I appreciate them after being in a place like Los Angeles where you have fair-weather friends. I can't even call them friends. They were associates.

When I lost my car, the associates disappeared. I soon realized that Los Angeles is a place where everyone was selfishly out for their dreams. They were not intentionally trying to cause harm, but when it came down to their dream or me, I was prepared to be run over or pushed aside. I felt like the victim in all of it, but in reality, I was the villain to my family. I was doing to them what was done to me. Sitting there and taking time to think, I saw my part in it all. My family didn't invite me to things anymore because they figured I wouldn't come. Why? Every time they invited me, I turned it down either because I needed to work or because I couldn't afford it. I didn't want them to know I wasn't making it. I wanted to thrive and come home as a Hollywood actress. I was ashamed that nothing was happening. I stopped bothering to go home because I didn't want people to see that I had nothing after years of being in California. I decided that day that I was going to leave. I wasn't going to hide anymore in a place that sucked me in. I had people who cared about me and loved me, Chantel, whether I was rich or poor.

I let those in the complex know that I was moving. I sold all my furniture that day and got rid of everything else. I returned my keys to Paul and thanked him for opening the doors and helping me. I asked Todd if I could stay for the night, and he said yes. I slept on his couch the night before my flight. I'd had a sense of stability for two years, but I knew it was time to go. The following morning, Todd dropped me off in his black stretch limo at Los Angeles International Airport for the exit of a lifetime.

My most significant moment was realizing my whole life was in a suitcase. I went to check in, and all I had was one bag. I reminisced on all of my sacrifices and all the family events that I missed. I had nothing to show for the ten years I spent in Los Angeles but the same suitcase I started with. I had nothing to show for my dreams but failure. I didn't regret going after my dreams, but I felt guilty for all the time I spent away from my family. If I took anything from Los Angeles, it was the wisdom and maturity that I gained.

It was one of the most emotional flights I had been on. As the airplane took off, my mind drifted as I looked out the window and into the clouds. I remembered the sex trafficking, domestic violence in my relationship, the car accident, homelessness, and losing my second car. As we climbed higher, I was mentally in a low place. Ten years of my life were gone, and it was on rapid replay during that five-hour flight to Baltimore/Washington International Airport.

I initially wanted to go to New York after talking with Brayden, but I had a change of heart. I decided to take a break before going to another major city. I urgently needed one. I was still hungry for my dreams, but my thirst for family outweighed it. I tried to encourage myself to have the resilience and strength to push through and still stand by thinking about the successes in Los Angeles. When God sent miracle money and destiny helpers, it wasn't a Hollywood success, but it meant a lot to me. The smile on my face faded because it was hard to be happy when the only thing I had to show for commending myself was one suitcase.

Moving back to D.C. wasn't as hard as I anticipated, but I didn't have a leg to stand on. I didn't have the finances to get my own place or a job, but I had God and my family. I had provisions through them that I didn't have in California. No one yelled or abused me. They sincerely took care of all my needs and asked for nothing in return. I slept at my great-grandparent's house. They were so happy to see me, and I was overjoyed to be with them. We didn't skip a beat. Once they told me where I would be sleeping, I was a wreck. I was in the room where I'd grown up. Opening my suitcase to unpack, I remembered packing it up to leave in the beginning. I was so emotional because I imagined I'd be this big movie star when I returned. I would be the one providing. I can say one thing about my great-grandparents, they never made me feel ashamed of the road that life had taken me. They never made me feel like a failure. One thing my great-grandfather always taught me was that failure is never final. I cried many times while in D.C., but his words carried me through some of my most challenging days.

I was embarrassed driving around in my great grandma's old Ford Taurus. In Los Angeles, everyone had nice cars. Although my first car was a lemon, my second car was a luxury car. How dare I feel bad for being in this car? I had no reason to complain because I was walking or riding a bike to get everywhere there. The problem was whenever I pulled myself up, something would be waiting for me around the corner. Within the first month of moving back, I was helping out with taking my younger cousin to school. The last person I expected to see was Allen. I ran into him on the street while with my cousin. One month before, Allen had a huge wedding that distant friends felt they needed to tell me about. Ironically, I had seen it happening in a dream months prior, so I was much more prepared than they realized.

When I saw him, he stopped to speak. We discussed that he had gotten married, and I told him I was happy for him. It was true that I was delighted for him. I believe that you should want the best for people when you genuinely love them, even when it hurts. I congratulated him, walked to the car, and sat there for a minute. I behaved well in front of him, but inside, I was in turmoil. It was ironic that I would see him walking down the street in D.C. When I was out of his eye distance, I cried. I let go of what he did to me, good and bad. In my heart, I was settled with him being married. A mutual friend contacted me the week I left Los Angeles and told me Allen was getting married. Their intentions in telling me were unclear. Were they trying to hurt me or inform me so I wouldn't be sideswiped?

I made peace with it because I said I'd never see him again. I grasped the fact that he was not the person God intended me to be with. God had way better in store for me. Once I acknowledged that Allen was my past and my future was brighter, I had no words. I was in a better place without him.

I couldn't sit around the house and needed to get on my feet. It was easier to secure a job when I did not have to worry about bills, housing, food, and transportation. As an associate minister I was placed in rotation to preach along with other ministers at my church. I made roughly $200 each time I was allowed the opportunity to preach. I eventually stepped down as a youth minister out of fear that I was not equipped to be the fiery preacher I thought I once could be. To be honest I wasn't ready. My second sermon I was incredibly nervous and felt my sermon wasn't impactful. I applied for a medical receptionist position because that was my last workplace. I was hired as one at Rockville Internal Medicine Group in Potomac, Maryland. I was moving forward, but being in my old room reminded me of what I hadn't accomplished, and I needed to find a new place. I relocated close by with my aunt and rented her basement. I wanted to be near my great-grandparents but wanted to give them their space. My aunt had a mattress. That's all she could offer me. There was no bed frame, and I couldn't afford one. I was on a mattress, on the floor, with no real clothes, but that was enough for me. I hadn't spent time building relationships with my family. I was so enthralled with my dreams and aspirations that I missed real family moments. My family knew things hadn't gone well for me in Los Angeles and that I needed refuge. It was clear to me there's nothing like family!

My best friend, Terry, another Baltimore School for the Arts classmate, called me to check in and see how family life was treating me. I told him about everything since I returned.

He told me, "You need to come to New York. You need to get out of D.C. You cannot just continue to go on unhappy."

I was going deeper into depression simply because I was not where I wanted to be in life. I could not see how ministry could tie into my passion for entertainment. I still deeply wanted to be in the arts.

He was right. I began to be a little overwhelmed by his response. Sometimes it takes a person from the outside looking in to see you. How could I continue to uplift others when I was so broken? My dreams were on hold. This was supposed to be a break for me, but it was instead breaking me. My faith in myself was shattered. It was easy being home, but I was still living day to day without aiming for a target. It reminded me of being in the apartment and Paul taking care of half the rent by discounting me monthly while I worked. It was a cycle, and it was time to end it.

Terry concluded by saying, "When you get here, I got you."

After our conversation, I started planning to move to New York. My two-month time frame turned into eight months in D.C. Terry was in New York in his final year at the New School studying theatre, and I trusted him. I decided it was time to leave.

I told my aunt I was moving to New York within a month. I was secure in my decision. All I had was a word and a prayer that it would work out. I randomly declared I would live in Williamsburg, Brooklyn and have a two-bedroom apartment. I was speaking my new life into existence. The Bible says that faith without works is dead, and I needed to do the work. New York wasn't that far away, so I got a ticket to ride the bus. I arrived at the Greyhound bus station and took the 6 a.m. ride on Saturday morning. The first thing I needed to live in New York was a job. I got off the bus, went straight to Brooklyn, and entered the William Vale Hotel.

I confidently walked in and dropped off my resume. I approached one of the staff members and asked if I could speak with a manager.

They asked me to wait for a few minutes, and then a beautiful Hispanic woman named Melissa came out and asked, "What do you want?"

Her New York accent was strong enough to knock down bricks. I politely said, "I'm looking for a job. Can I meet with you?"

She guided me over to a couch in the lobby. As we sat down, she replied, "It's funny because we're looking for a front desk agent. What experience do you have?"

Was this happening? I had to pull it together and answer because this may be the job.

"I worked in room service at the Four Seasons in Beverly Hills."

Melissa looked at me and asked, "Can you start on Monday?"

I was jumping on the inside, but kept my poise on the outside.

"I can start on Monday," I quickly replied.

She said, "Okay, welcome to the William Vale Hotel. I have some paperwork for you, and after that, I will see you on Monday."

I had a job. God has a way of using all of your past for your future. Working at the Four Seasons once again opened a door for me. Just when I thought Los Angeles was for nothing, God showed me how He can use a situation that we see as bad for our good. I was on cloud nine, and then I was smacked back into time. I had to be at work in two days in another state, and all of my belongings were still in D.C. I also did not live in New York. There wasn't an apartment to call home.

I immediately had to return on the bus to my aunt's place to collect my suitcase. I was moving on pure faith that I would have it all by the end of the month. I had this presentiment that I belonged in New York. So many members of my Baltimore School for the Arts Ensemble lived there. I considered a few of them like Brayden to be my family. He was running the Public theater at the time. And there was Terry, who was in film school. There were so many others who started out with me and were thriving in the Big Apple. I knew that by living there, I could perform my craft with many available opportunities.

But where was I going to stay when I went back? My friends told me they had me, but I didn't want to interrupt their lives. I needed a place close to the hotel. I searched the internet and found a room on Airbnb in Bed-Stuy. I was clueless about Brooklyn or any of the different boroughs in New York. All I knew was that I had a job offer and had to report back on Monday. Before I left D.C., I received my last paycheck from Rockville Internal Medicine Group that Friday, so I told myself I must take this job. I was figuring it out as I went.

Melissa's last words before I left were, "You must be here on Monday morning. You better be here on time."

I didn't want to risk the chance of losing my spot. I purchased another ticket back to New York, and

I packed my suitcase once again. The way I left Los Angeles would be the same way I left D.C. God and the suitcase. That's all I needed.

I didn't have enough money to Uber to Williamsburg, so I promptly figured out how to take the New York subway. There needed to be more time to learn the entire transport system, which I knew was the only way to survive there. I used wisdom in my choices from my many years in Los Angeles. I had to use the public transportation system there because I didn't have a car.

I made it to work Monday morning on time, just as Melissa had asked. Once I got settled in and worked my first two weeks, I was getting to know my coworkers. I asked them and others around my new job if they knew anybody who needed a roommate. Nobody knew anyone who was searching, but they directed me to an app called Roomi. It lists people looking for a roommate in a specific area. I had never used or heard of it before that day, but I downloaded it to check it out.

Since I knew my job was in Williamsburg, I looked for a place there. I didn't want to be too far from work or the trains. My money from my last paycheck was running low, and my time was running out at my Airbnb. Although I could continue to stay there, it was getting expensive. I didn't want to keep spending money on an Airbnb when I could pay rent in a permanent place. I also had to purchase food and other necessities and was budgeting what I had left. I would need every penny to move into at least a room somewhere with what I had left until I received my first paycheck. I wanted a two-bedroom in Williamsburg, but it was unrealistic for me and where I was financially. These are the reasons I tried Roomi, which turned out to be a great way to find a place. I set up meetings with different potential roommates on days I was off work as I took my next step forward.

I hadn't been in New York long, but I knew I liked it. My job seemed to be working out, and knowing others there made it even more comfortable for me. There were a lot of great apartments, but I needed to make sure it would be affordable for me in the long run. After my roommate experience in California, my outlook changed on how I chose. Although the apartment might fit my price range, I paid attention to the person I would be sharing a space with. I didn't want a repeat of the Los Angeles experience.

CHAPTER 6

The Rain of My Tears

SOMETIMES YOU HAVE TO BE YOUR OWN TISSUE.

– Chantel Dean

I ENCOUNTERED A FEW PEOPLE WITH GREAT apartments, but one woman lived the closest to my job. I went to her house to see the condition it was in and if it was an atmosphere I could live in. It was 106 Marcy Avenue, apartment number two, right by the Williamsburg Bridge. The cross street was South Second, Marcy. It was only a twenty minute walk to the William Vale Hotel. I wanted to be within walking distance so that I could save money and not have to rely on

Uber or the train. Walking wouldn't be the worst thing, and I had been here before. This was the state of New York, where people walked everywhere. I wasn't out of place having to do so.

The young lady invited me to her home. A bed was already there because her former roommate had just moved out and didn't want to take the bed. This was perfect for me because I had no furniture. I had come from a mattress on the floor in D.C., and as long as I had a roof over my head, it was fine.

While listening to her, I said to myself, *"This might be the place for me. It already comes with a bed."*

This was the winner. As I walked around, she showed me the tiniest-looking room. It had to be a person's walk-in closet.

She told me, "Nope, that is the room. Welcome to New York."

Her name was Heather a Canadian girl, and I told her I wanted to stay there. I did not get an immediate yes. I would have to wait for her answer. She said she would tell me if it was mine by the next day. I couldn't sleep, hoping it was the place. The following morning, I was anxious wondering if it would be my new home. I was sure I wasn't the only one searching for a place and was praying she didn't choose someone else. I went on to work and did my normal shift. As I was walking away from my desk, Heather called.

I took the call discreetly, and she asked, "Do you want the place? If so, you can move in May."

Of course, I wanted the place. I told her, "Yes."

I was so excited knowing that I was working, and by the end of the month, I would have a place. I had one room and she had the other, but it was still a two-bedroom. On May 1st, I moved into 106 Marcy Avenue with Heather.

Heather had been in the fashion business for many years after attending the New School for Fashion in New York. She worked for the Gap creating accessories. The apartment was her home. She had lived there for ten years and housed many roommates throughout the years. It was a beautiful apartment with a patio. I was happy to have a roof over my head and be close to work. My biggest worries were resolved, and all I needed was bed sheets. There was no need for other furniture because all that could fit in that tiny room was a bed, a small chair, and a nightstand. I signed a lease with her and decided this was perfect for me. She gave me a key and told me the rent was due on the first.

"Welcome to your new home," she said with enthusiasm.

I enjoyed my room and felt like this was my home. I no longer had to stay in an Airbnb, hoping my time wouldn't run out. I had a real place.

I began to get to know Heather and asked her

about her birthday. It was June 14. We had grown so close that I invited her to spend her birthday at the hotel. Her mom came into town, and I told her to join us. I left the front desk and went to sing to her. I sang happy birthday while presenting Heather with a bottle of wine. It was her 37th birthday. She and her mother enjoyed every minute of it. It was definitely a birthday to remember. We began to spend a lot more time together at home. We did face masks together and even talked about past relationships. We got along well, and she shared some of her favorite places to go and shows to see.

No one could visit New York and ignore a Broadway show! I found myself going as often as I could. I was way more inspired in New York than I ever was in Los Angeles. I had access to all these places, including Broadway. I also had my friends. Brayden was a producer at the Public theater, and he would gift me tickets so I could see shows for free. One that stands out was *For Colored Girls Who Have Considered Suicide/When the Rainbow is Enuf.* Being able to see that on the stage was life-changing. I was grateful for the connections God gave me in New York. I was able to work and play. I was seeing friends from the Baltimore School for the Arts that I had not seen in more than ten years.

It was becoming a regular occurrence to run into someone and realize I started out with them. Baltimore

School for the Arts was one of the safest places I had ever been. I felt the protection I had been missing since 2008. Before leaving for Los Angeles, security came from the people who wanted the best for me and loved me. I lost that after dealing with so many people who hurt and abandoned me in Los Angeles. New York was different. The city treated me wonderfully. I felt alive and motivated. I became a real New Yorker and saw myself staying indefinitely.

I started attending Brooklyn Tabernacle. At the beginning of August, there was a tug on my heart to get back to God, my first love. I'd left the church for a while and began looking for one. Growing up in church, I missed the fellowship. Sunday mornings in the car listening to gospel music with my great-grandparents were the best. I'd always heard of the Brooklyn Tabernacle choir because it was the only music I was allowed to listen to in their presence. Songs such as "Order My Steps" had been on my playlist for many years, so I knew it was the church for me.

I needed to go to church, but oddly, in the first week of August, I knew I *had* to go. It was very random because while living there, church hadn't crossed my mind. This was mainly due to the excitement of New York and conflicting work schedules. I was so distracted by the bright lights that I was forgetting about the light of the world (John 8:12). There was a pressure to get my life right with God and make it to church every Sunday. Battling a spirit of rebellion regarding my calling and church attendance throughout the years had led me here, but this call was different. I could not ignore it or shake it. I walked into Brooklyn Tabernacle church, and my life was never the same.

After church, I returned home on fire for God. I hadn't been to a service since stepping down as the youth minister of my great-grandfather's church. I knew I was called to preach, but I wasn't ready to give up the world to do it. Culture had a way of pulling me in and keeping me away from God. I walked into that apartment on Marcy Ave with tears in my eyes because as always, God was working everything out in my life. I returned home with a spirit of total praise. The Holy Spirit was strong on me, and I couldn't let go. I was letting God take over. I was aware that Heather may not have believed what I did, but I had to testify.

I never wanted to be one of those people who threw their religion on others, and Heather and I were only roommates, but I couldn't hold it in.

I kept saying, "God is so good."

I was moving around and talking about God and the things He brought me through. I was on fire for the Lord and couldn't help it. I was in our home singing about Jesus. I didn't check to see if Heather was home or not because the glory of the Lord could not be contained. Heather came out of her room when she heard me.

She said, "You're in a really good mood!"

I looked at her and said, "Heather, I just came from church, and it was a good service. I just feel on fire for the Lord right now. God is so good."

From that, Heather and I engaged in this profound conversation about God. I asked her if she knew Jesus and how much He loved us. That afternoon, we spoke for two hours about God and how she would start attending church with me. All of this happened because God told me to start taking Sundays off, and I obeyed. I didn't feel like it was my place to have a conversation about Jesus with her before then, but that day, it was different. Something happened when I returned home from church that first week of August 2019, and I had to engage with her.

I returned to work Monday morning and reiterated to the manager that I needed every Sunday off due to my religious reasons. I knew that I needed to attend church. She agreed, and I followed my normal work routine. When I returned home that evening, I began to talk to Heather about our daily events. She mentioned a guy named Blake, whom she'd previously dated on and off. I hadn't met him before then, but I remembered his name. Blake was a graffiti artist in New York who had gotten into a bad motorcycle accident.

According to Heather, his mom was a minister. She prayed over him, and he made a full recovery. This was another nugget given to Heather to get her wheels turning about God.

She said, "I've heard about the Lord. I want to start attending church with you."

I heard her heart and told her, "Heather, you must come to this church with me this Sunday."

Another week passed, and Heather still had not gone to church with me. On August 25, 2019, I woke up ready for church. I got dressed and walked into the living room and saw Heather sitting on the couch.

I said, "Hey Heather, I'm going to church. Are you still coming?"

She mentioned she had a lot of laundry to do, but she would come next Sunday. She was too tired. I knew it was because of Blake. He came over on Saturday night. I immediately felt a lousy presence about him because of what she told me about him. He dated Heather on and off while he married someone else. When he did come around, he treated Heather poorly throughout their entire relationship. I'd grown a little protective over her. I could see myself in her from having dated Allen and how I stayed in a relationship that hurt me. Blake was showing back up, and she was letting him in. She was such a nice person, but he was shady. She returned from spending the night out with him and was exhausted.

She spoke to me with all her energy and said, "I want to go to church with you, but I'm so tired."

"It's okay, don't worry about it, maybe next Sunday," I told her as I left for church and as she lay down to sleep.

Everything was finally aligning for me. Church brought another joy to my life that filled a void. Although I had friends and was in a good place, having God made my life top tier. I believed I could have all I was pursuing. A friend of mine invited me to the Afropunk concert held in Brooklyn every year with many different performers and performances. Heather once again turned me down for church because she was tired. After church, I came home and changed my clothes. Before leaving, I noticed Heather was still in her bed. Her feet were hanging off the bed, and I thought she was knocked out from a late night with Blake. I assumed that was how she slept and didn't pay much attention to her. If she was that tired, I wasn't going to bother her. I opened the door when my friend came. I was putting on the last finishes to my outfit, and we left for the concert.

It was great, and we had the best time together. I stayed at my friend's house that night because I only had to work on Monday evening. I was worn out from having a good ole New York time. I got back home at 6 a.m. I flopped right on my bed to get some rest. I was knocked out until it was time to get ready for work. When I was on my way to the bathroom to get ready, I could see in Heather's room. She had transparent doors with a see-through sheet that was tied up. She looked to be still asleep. I thought she must be exhausted to be still knocked out. It wasn't registering with me that something could be wrong. I presumed she must have taken the day off because she partied too hard. I got dressed quietly for work and left. I was off work at 11:30 p.m. because I went in later than usual. I walked in, and the place was dark. Heather's room was dark. That was unlike her because usually when I came home, she would be watching TV in the living room. I went to bed thinking she was sleeping and would go to work the next day.

My life was hit again on August 27, 2019. I was used to hearing Heather get ready for work on weekday mornings with her moving about the apartment and shuffling dishes. On that Tuesday morning, I hadn't heard anything and began to worry. This was strange behavior for Heather, who wasn't following her routine. I was in bed trying to fall back to sleep for over an hour, but for some reason, I could not. Something inside of me told me I should go into her room and check on her to ensure she was okay. She usually walked out the door at 9 a.m. to take the A train into the city. I was fighting myself to check on her. I began to try to tell myself that she was okay. *She's going to get up in a second. I'm clearly overreacting. I'm being overprotective of my roommate. She told me she was tired on Sunday. She partied on Saturday with Blake. I'm just being paranoid at this point. She'll be up any minute now.*

I was extremely uncomfortable at 9 a.m. She rarely missed work, and she wasn't getting prepared. The first thing I did was call a friend.

"I'm kind of scared. I haven't seen my roommate for about three days. I saw her and spoke to her on Sunday. She told me she was tired and was going to lay down. I haven't seen her since then. I believe she's still in the room, but I want someone on the phone before I panic and call the police."

My friend stayed on the phone as I thought, *Chantel, you're crazy. Why are you overreacting? Clearly, open the door and say Heather. She's taking a nap. She's taking some time off because she's tired.*

When I approached the door, all my nerves kicked in. I peeked down and realized her feet were turning purple. I kept trying to rationalize that there had to be another explanation until the last second. We have a patio. That's it. She went on the patio without shoes and her feet were dirty.

With my story in mind, I opened the door. Heather looked like she was sleeping. She was face down and her feet were hanging off the bed, the same way they were on Monday. Before proceeding any further, I opened the door to our apartment. If she was dead, I was going to freak out and run out of the apartment.

I walked back and opened her bedroom door saying, "Heather," in almost a whisper the first time. I didn't want to surprise her by being loud if she was asleep. Every time I'd say her name and not hear a response, I would get louder and louder. I was screaming, and the people underneath and above us heard me.

I hung up on my friend and ran into the hallway to dial 911. I didn't know what to do. All I could say was, "Please, my God, my roommate is not responding."

The dispatcher was telling me to do things like check her pulse and see if she was breathing. I wasn't going to do any of that. She was gone. I was not touching her body. I screamed.

"Just send somebody! I'm scared, and you need to come right now."

I stayed in the hallway pacing. What was I supposed to do? I was not going in there. Minutes later, I heard sirens coming down the street. I felt a sense of relief and met the emergency response team downstairs. Suddenly, there were all these firemen, police, and EMS workers. They asked me to lead them to her and followed me upstairs. The EMS team entered the room and lifted Heather's completely stiff body. I could see that she was dead and rigor mortis had occurred. It finally hit me. I started screaming at the top of my lungs and crying hysterically. I knew the answer but asked anyway.

I looked at the EMS and said, "Is she dead?"

They all looked at me, shaking their heads in agreement. Yes. Soon after, police officers and detectives surrounded me in that tiny two-bedroom apartment in Williamsburg. Detective Ducharme firmly said, "Sit down. We have to ask you some questions."

Finding Heather dead was one of the most traumatic experiences. I was devastated, confused, and in shock. Even with all my emotions, I had to answer questions and calls from her job because she hadn't been to work. I had to tell her immediate family the devastating news. The hardest thing I ever had to do was explain to Heather's mother that her child was gone. Hearing the screams and disbelief while you are living it is a pain I never want to know again. I will never forget that day I lost a great friend. Hours later I received a call from Heather's mother that the reason for her passing was from a drug overdose and that she had died instantly.

I spoke to my friend, Terry, who left his classes at the New School for the day to console me. He allowed me to stay the night at his apartment in Brooklyn. I couldn't stay in the apartment that night. It would be too much knowing Heather died there. I told my employer what happened and that I needed some time off. I ultimately decided to get on the first train from

Penn Station to Union Station in D.C. I took off two weeks for bereavement and went home to my family. I wanted the comfort of my great-grandparents. I had to strategize what I would do next. Would I stay in New York, or would I leave? If I left, where would I go? What about the job I had? Where would I stay if I went back?

Upon arriving home in D.C., problems were waiting for me there as well. My mom had lost her job at the Metro, and all her belongings were outside her home because she was evicted. I drove my great-grandmother's car to help gather her belongings. She had nowhere to go, and I asked if she wanted to come to New York with me. She agreed. My great-grandparents allowed her to move in with them that day due to her job loss and eviction until she would leave with me.

Evening came, and I ran to the arms of members of my hometown congregation at Mount Zion Baptist Church. I went the next day to Wednesday night bible study led by my great-grandfather, Pastor John W. Davis. I was in shock and trying to understand what had just happened. I wanted a word from God, understanding, and to move from the spirit of fear. I received all that I came for and more. Over the next two weeks, I saw therapists in Maryland and did my best to assemble the pieces of my life. I felt an immense amount of guilt over Heather's death. Maybe I could have saved her if I had just made her go to church that day, even though she said she was tired. I could have checked on her Saturday night when she came in. Why did this happen to her? Why did this happen to me? It was devastating to know that I would never see her again. When I returned to New York, I would no longer hear her music or her getting ready for work. It changed the way I looked at life. People always say life is short but don't always understand how short it actually is. You can be here today and gone tomorrow. Heather was a proud Canadian girl who had big dreams and goals like the rest of us. From that moment on, I decided I would not waste another moment holding grudges, procrastinating, or living in fear.

I often think of Heather and pray for friends and family who knew her well. Her death was a significant turning point in my life. It made me value my own life more, but I still felt survivor's guilt. I continued therapy through Better Help online, wondering if there was anything I could have done to save her. I was able to get a different point of view and sound advice from someone who was far from the situation. I believe God intended for me to go to the Brooklyn Tabernacle and return on fire for the Lord that Sunday. I shared what I had learned about Jesus and Heather was receptive.

I believe God allowed her to accept Jesus as her savior before calling her home. Knowing that kept me going. God loved her, and she was able to surrender to Him.

God nudged me at the right time to attend church that day because He knew what she needed from Him. The only way she would have trusted God at the time was coming through me. Thank you, Lord, for that.

My two-week mental break was ending, and I knew I had to return to work and the apartment in Brooklyn. I kissed my great-grandparents goodbye and left with my mother. We headed to Union Station in D.C. at 6 a.m. to return to Penn Station in New York. We spent three hours on the Amtrak train. The ride seemed to never end, especially not knowing what to expect on the other side. My mother also had a suitcase with as many things as possible to start a new life. I had a small bag because most of my things were in the apartment. My great-grandparents had told me that they really couldn't care for my mom anymore. They were older, and she needed much more than they could handle. I made the choice that was best for everyone involved. It would be most beneficial for us to be together in New York.

CHAPTER 7

The Scattered Showers of My Dreams

WHEN PLAN B HAS ANOTHER PLAN FOR ME, I LEAN ON GOD.

— *Chantel Dean*

When Heather died, her mom contacted me and said she was going to come to the apartment to handle things. She was supposed to be there for a week or two. I wanted to give her space to do what she needed to do and grieve for her daughter. I also needed space to grieve Heather in my own way. I returned to Marcy Avenue on the train two weeks after Heather's death with my mother. I was scared to return to New York alone because I didn't know what would be on the other side of the apartment door. I walked up the stairs with my Bible in hand, reciting Psalm 27. When I opened the door, everything was still the same as on the morning of August 27. I couldn't stand the thought of silence, so I turned on the television that was still sitting there in the living room. Ironically, a funeral home commercial came on. I immediately shut it off because it was too eerie. My mom and I unpacked and settled in for the night. It was too hard to pack up anything of Heather's that was left, so I didn't for the first few days. Eventually, I would have to because no one from her family would be able to come and do it. They were grieving, and I understood.

I had to go back to work at the William Vale Hotel. My bereavement time was up, and for me to continue to pay rent, I had to keep my job. I couldn't hide away from the world forever. I went back to my job two days after returning to New York. I was doing my normal work routine until I looked up. I was shocked to see Blake, Heather's ex, whom she had last been with before her death. He walked up to the front desk. He explained to me that he stayed with a friend at the hotel after his wife kicked him out and asked if he could move in and be my roommate.

Was he insane? How dare he ask me that after all that

just happened? Heather was my friend, and I was still grieving her. Why wasn't he?

Those were the thoughts I wanted to say, but I didn't. I held my composure. There was no need to fight this battle. God would do that. I knew Heather was too good for him. He was a graffiti artist with a history of drugs, and I wanted nothing to do with him. He told me that he would be there for the next two days. I found a picture of them together while packing the last of Heather's photos. When I went to work the next day, I handed it to him and said it was best not to speak to me anymore.

I was still trying to grapple with the reality of finding her dead, and it seemed like every day had a new challenge. It was easy when my mom was in the house with me, but there were traumatizing moments when I looked at Heather's door. I could still see her lying there, with purple feet hanging over the bedside. Over the next few weeks, I cleaned up her items around the apartment, but when I picked something up, it reminded me of her. Whether it was an outfit she wore to work or to go out in, it would bring up a memory. After gathering all her things, I packed and shipped her personal items and photos to her mother. I was hurting for her because to lose a daughter so soon had to be hard. I was glad for the limited time I spent with Heather, who was a jewel. I tried to return to my life as it was before, but

I couldn't. Heather's presence seemed to still be all over the apartment. Her things were gone, but memories of her were not. I found myself constantly in a non stop flow of tears. Although death is a natural part of life, I don't believe it's easy to deal with. Grief is hard. The amount of time needed to heal depends on whether the person is young or seasoned. When in my room, there always seemed to be constant thoughts of death and life in the back of my mind. Sometimes, it takes the most crushing moments to bring you closer to God.

Returning to New York, I had to act like nothing happened. I had to touch Heather's things, knowing she would never use them again or be there to get them herself. It was mentally stressful. I had to live in a space where someone passed away as I slept. I was flooded with all of these emotions while moving my mom in. My mental health was being challenged in more ways than one. My mom has always suffered from mental illness—bipolar schizophrenia to be exact. It has always affected our relationship. My mom was now living full-time with me, and I had to navigate this new life as a caretaker and daughter. I felt it was best for my mom to sleep in Heather's room.

To make it livable, I first had to establish with the landlord a payment plan. Since Heather rented from him, I took over the full payments. I made swift arrangements after Heather's items were removed. I hired professional cleaners and bought brand-new furniture for the room. I also purchased some new clothes for my mom. I bought a Frenchie and named her Rosé. That was my drink of choice at the time. She acted as my emotional support animal to help me stay at the apartment without having multiple panic attacks from thinking of what transpired. I left my previous dog Danger in Los Angeles with Todd, he had reminded me of Allen and had formed a genuine bond with Todd. Having my mom there was helpful because I wouldn't be alone. I wasn't sure that I could handle that. Although I knew she was sick, I could handle this. I would rather take on the task of having her with me and dealing with my New York life than leave her with my great-grandparents, whom I knew could not care for her.

I had transformed the apartment into a much cleaner, lighter space by praying over it, having it cleaned, and redecorating. Within three months, my mom got a job at Trader Joe's, and it seemed like she loved New York. She was becoming more acclimated to living in the Big Apple. Soon after she got settled in, I was contacted by a producer I'd previously met while living in Los Angeles. It seemed that my dreams were beginning to find me again. I was a creative person who would act, sing, or dance. I wasn't bound to one craft and wanted to explore my options. I could still be a big star, and having a footing in New York could push me there. He mentioned we should do some music together, and I thought it would be good for me to take a trip and get out of the apartment. I knew my mom would be okay by herself, and she also had my dog to keep her company.

So after three months of acclimating to New York, I flew to Los Angeles. I wasn't thinking about all the bad things that happened to me there because I was in a new place in life. I had a job and a place. This would be a roundtrip flight. I wouldn't give up anything to see what he could do for me. Once in Los Angeles, I met with the producer and recorded my first songs ever. The studio was cozy and located in North Hollywood. It was dimly lit with LED wall lights, providing a sense of creativity. The session lasted from 9 p.m. to 3 a.m., which is typical for studio times. After recording the spoken word song, we played around with some beats and recorded two rap songs. I went to record a spoken word album, but it quickly turned into making rap songs, and they came out well.

When I returned to New York City, I was in the clouds. Everything was looking up for me. I had a change in purpose. I was going to be a music artist and push my music career. New York would be the best place to do it. There were so many record labels based in the city. Rapping is what I was going to put my energy into. I had tried acting for so long in Los Angeles, and doors weren't opening. When I heard myself after recording the song, I felt this was it! It's a shame how quickly we can forget about God after He brings us through a storm. Everything I knew about God bringing me out and providing for me was thrown away. I made raunchy, curse-filled songs that didn't reflect the actual calling of God on my life. My music wasn't going to bring anyone to Christ. It was for the culture, and at that moment, that's all I cared about. I was finally going to make it in a big city, and everyone would know my name.

My great-grandmother would always quote to me the verse that states, "What does it profit a man to gain the world and lose his soul?"

I knew I was making music that would not please my great-grandparents. It was secular, and God was nowhere to be found in it. After going to Los Angeles, I created this persona, Telli Dean. It still wasn't clicking to me that I couldn't even be myself. I was putting on this alter ego to be someone I wasn't. I became obsessed with making it in the music industry and getting fame. Going to church and focusing on God was put on the back burner. After everything being at church helped me with, I tossed it to the side. I didn't want to spend my Sundays walking into church and hearing about the glory of God. I wanted to party and hang out. I had it all. I had money, a place, a music career, and friends in high places in New York. Who needed to seek God? I was distracting myself with people and things. It was the glimmer of the party life, music events, and award shows. The nightlife was fun and exciting. God started to become boring to me. I had everything I prayed for, so why keep going to God?

There were so many places to be in New York, and I came across a unique find. It was an event that, for a fee, would put me in front of reputable A&Rs from major record labels. I paid the price, and it indeed put me in front of the big wigs. The room gave me a *wow* feeling. I was in front of the people who had the power to sign me. They'd listened to my music when I was auditioning, and it seemed to be a good choice for me. This was my first time going to Quad Studios in Times Square. They always seemed to have this particular event there with the prominent people from the top labels in New York. Myself and a host of other individuals were there, hoping they would pick us up. We were all in suspense, and they heard our sound and decided if they wanted to sign us. I had great music for someone who was an amateur.

As I climbed up the ladder during the event, I was able to get directly to entertainment executives. There were two I had the pleasure to meet, but one in particular seemed so interested in me. For someone who had just decided to be in this world, this was a dream come true.

The more interested executive said to me, "Hey, take my number. Let's keep in touch."

The 300 people in front of me all wished for someone like him to give them contact information. From the beginning, he seemed very genuine. Meeting him, I never felt that he would be anything other than a great person. He invited me to come to his office the next day. I left the event knowing that I was the next artist to be released. All things were working in my favor. I had never gone to such events prior to that day, and my first time there I was approached for my music by a big-time executive. I went home with a vision of what was in store for me. As I got up the next morning, he took me to tour major record label offices. Technically, I was a nobody in the industry. I spent ten years trying to be somebody in Los Angeles. I was now in New York before A&R's getting walked in for meetings. I was the somebody I waited all those years to be.

Everything seemed to be going great. We finally made it to his office. I gifted him a lovely painting that I purchased for him, which I wanted to be remembered for. The first impression is always the lasting one. He also gave me a bottle of D'usse Cognac. Afterward, he invited me to the studio. I decided to go since the day had been so amazing. We left the label office and while

I was waiting for a car to pull up for us like in the movies, he ordered an Uber to take us to the studio. I felt so special as I watched people standing outside waiting to give him their mixtape. I walked to the car, knowing I wasn't one of them. I didn't have to stand outside in the cold and wait for this man to recognize me. I was with him. He gave me a tour of the label, and I was getting to jump in the car with him and get this special treatment. I knew that I was going to make it, and he was going to see to it that I did.

It didn't take long before I found out that he was way more interested in me sexually than my music. In our first two meetings, he was able to mask his true intentions. He was nice and discussed my career. I saw who he truly was when we did a studio session with an artist he was working with. Things started to get weird with him, and I started to find myself in compromising positions with some of the most prominent music executives. I found out about this "dark side of the industry." It is the part no one wants to talk about. Whether it is because of fear or shame, I'm not completely sure, but it's not known unless you are in certain circles or have been a victim yourself. A lot of A&Rs are predators who use their position to sexually harass and push women into corners for the sake of making it in the industry.

I had heard about these kinds of things, but he seemed to be someone who had it all. Why would he want to do that to me? The way it started, he seemed so interested in my music. I'd been in his office and was grateful for a significant label taking interest in me, but that wasn't the case. He began to sexually harass me for over two months. There were incessant text messages, and he would send me private pictures of himself. At first, I ignored him. When that no longer worked, I told him that I wasn't interested. He completely cut off all communication with me after that. I was hurt that I lost my opportunity, but I had standards. I wasn't going to lower them for fame. I went back to the drawing board because I was determined to make it. I'd meet another A&R, the same way I came across him, but would they treat me right?

I focused back on my job but kept my career in the forefront. Months later, I received a private message on Instagram from a prominent label executive.

"I love your music, Big Telli. Would you be available to meet?"

I had no clue how, but this guy found me. I must be good, right? Why else would he have reached out when I wasn't even promoting my music? This was great. Maybe it didn't work out with the other label because it was supposed to work out with another prominent label. I was motivated all over again. He invited me to the office, but it would be late in the evening. I thought that was a bit odd. I was used to meeting people during the day. He was supposed to be meeting with an up-and-coming artist at the time. I knew that most artists spend hours in the studio, and it can be up until three in the morning before they would finish a song.

I found it a bit weird when I got buzzed up and walked inside the room. I looked around and noticed no one was there. He saw my facial expression and told me some people were there, but they had left. A high level of discomfort came over me because the lights were off, and people weren't there. He offered me a drink, and then he ended up sexually assaulting me. The emotional and psychological effects were immediate. I was filled with shame and embarrassment. I wanted to run out of his office, but I couldn't. He had locked me in. I felt so disgusted and taken advantage of. All I could do was wonder.

What the hell? Why is this industry like this?

As soon as I could leave, I did. I ran out and went straight home. I cried, remembering all the things I had gone through with sex trafficking. Although it wasn't the exact same way, it was the same experience. I thought I was over these types of men.

I blamed myself because how stupid could I be? I had already been through this once. Why was I so naive? This industry didn't want the best for me. Men were using their power and influence to abuse young women like me. That was my fault because I idolized them and forgot who had the real power to put me in the right position: God. I was on the road to ministry and getting right with God, and instead was running through the streets of New York crying. It was the breaking point I needed. It took that reminder of being taken advantage of to realize that as many times as I'd turned my back on God, He never turned His back on me.

My phone was again filled over the next few days with sexual images and messages from him. He was yet another music executive who tried to lure me into his despicable web. Did they speak to each other and choose to try me? He was way more persistent than the last. I had to delete my Instagram and ultimately went into hiding. It wasn't enough that he sexually assaulted me, but he kept calling my phone. Going straight to voicemail didn't stop him. I was unsure if he was afraid that I would tell the authorities or why he kept continuing to contact me. After a while, I changed my number. He would never get a chance to be around me again. I called a girlfriend of mine, and as soon as I heard her voice, I fell apart. I cried to her about how I'd been preyed upon. My desire to chase the world led me into a dark place. I thought I was different, and I smirked around all those people waiting in line to meet the major person I was with. I now wish I had been out there, and none of this had ever happened to me.

I fell into a severe depression with no control over it. No matter what I tried, there was no shaking it. I had moved to New York, my roommate died, and I had fallen for the illusion of fame. In my crying, I could feel God's love for me. My depression was wearing off, and I wanted nothing more to do with music or anything else at that point. I wanted my total focus back on God. I just walked around carrying the guilt of my decisions. What could have been done differently? I was just a girl from D.C. who had these big dreams. I moved to two major U.S. cities for entertainment, but all that did was take me further away from God. I finally knew what it was like to chase waterfalls. All these men only wanted sex, and it was so hurtful. They had people willing to give them what they wanted, but they would rather steal it from the unexpected youth who only wanted to trust them. I began to wonder how many of us don't say anything because we feel our voice doesn't matter compared to a successful person in a position of power? Who are we to them? Why are we afraid to speak up? What would happen to us if we did?

I had an internal battle with my why. Why did I turn away from God so quickly? Why was I always so easily led astray from God when it came to things of the world such as entertainment? This wasn't the first time I failed God, and it surely wouldn't be the last. The Bible states in Romans 3:23 that we all sin and fall short of the glory of God. I knew that I was called to be a preacher but honestly, I didn't see how the money would come from that. Would it be cool to do something like that? It wasn't glamorous to be a preacher. It was extraordinary to be an actress or a music star. God was trying to call me to something bigger, but I had my mind set on what I wanted.

My great-grandma would say to me, "Your arms are too short to box with God. You are running away from your true calling—ministry. You have to stop playing with God."

I had my "Jonah in the belly of the whale moment" in New York. Storms are never meant to destroy you but to redirect you. That was the case with Jonah, and that was certainly the case with me. Jonah tried to run from God, who had called him to be a prophet to Nineveh. Johah rebelled and fled across the sea in the opposite direction. God sent a storm to stop Johah, who was thrown overboard and into the belly of a whale. The story showed me that even when we disobey God, He still sends us a way back to Him. I realized I had pulled a Jonah repeatedly in my life and began to see just how patient God had been with me. The storms and trials were all a setup to see my actual value. It would never come from the world but ultimately from our Heavenly Father. Every mistake was a setup for better, even if I couldn't see it.

God is called the potter because He molds us and puts us back together. God does His best work in us when we're broken. The word says his power is made perfect in our weakness (2 Corinthians 12:9). I was tired because I was working on my own instead of relying on God's strength. I wanted to keep up with culture and trends more than I wanted to keep his commandments and instructions. Time and time again, it led me astray (Luke 17:33). I was tired of being tired, and I wanted Christ more than ever. How could He love me when I failed Him over and over? Did He even still hear me? I will never understand God's love because He never fails us, even when we fail Him. I felt like the prodigal son—dirty, lost,and guilt-ridden—only to realize my Father was waiting for me to return all along. I had to go out and party and waste my money on strange events and do all the things I did. If not, I would not have seen how dirty the industry was. I would have stayed and could have been in worse danger. If I weren't mistreated by men, I wouldn't understand the love of God. He loved me enough that He didn't allow me to invest much time in a place I was never supposed to be.

CHAPTER 8

The Torrent of a Pandemic

WHAT I TRIED TO HANDLE, HANDLED ME.
— *Chantel Dean*

I WAS FINALLY GETTING MY LIFE BACK ON TRACK as the year 2019 ended. The first few months of 2020, I felt a burst of new energy. I was slowly moving forward from the sexual assault and picking up the pieces of my life. I continued to work at the William Vale Hotel, checking clients in and trying to live a more God-centered life. Everything was going well until suddenly, the world shut down. It was March 2020, and people were becoming infected with COVID-19. We were entering into the era of the pandemic. I panicked like everyone else, trying to get toilet paper, towels, and adequate food. I was spending money on things for the unforeseen future, and then was told my job was shutting down. I wouldn't have an income and didn't know how long I would be out of work. The up side was my mom was still employed but not by choice. She was forced to stay on the job as an essential worker. She was ringing up hundreds of people daily at the Manhattan Trader Joe's.

In the middle of the shutdown, my brother, a medical doctor, was dealing with his crisis of being overworked. He was seeing so many patients suffering from the illness for which there was no cure. He became emotionally challenged, having to watch people come in and never leave. This was becoming a daily occurrence, and he was helpless without being able to prevent it from taking place. It was all a nightmare and a wake-up call. I was not immune, much like the rest of the world, and I contracted COVID-19 at the beginning of April. I became extremely ill and quarantined myself in a room away from my mom. I wanted to keep her safe and uninfected. I also didn't want her to lose her job because there was nothing but uncertainty due to COVID-19.

In addition to a global pandemic, racism, and police brutality seemed to be at an all-time high. At the beginning of 2020, I often found myself leading protests and crowds through the streets of Williamsburg with a megaphone while yelling the names George Floyd, Breonna Taylor, and Rayshard Brooks. This seemed like the only response we could give to the terrorism on Black lives. It was in our faces daily. Every time you turned on the news or social media, there were more senseless killings. We needed to stand up for ourselves, and I was going to ensure we were heard. Often officers in NYPD cars would follow us, but they didn't harm us. I would make my voice resonate through the streets of Brooklyn. I was so empowered by the movement that I began to use my musical talents to help. I was led to write a prolific remix of Kendrick Lamar's "King's Dead" about my idol, Dr. Martin Luther King, Jr., and the injustice against Black people. A group of my Baltimore School for the Arts tribe and I decided to create a music video. They encouraged me and acted as creative directors, producers, and actors for the project. We planned to record in D.C., so we packed our things and recorded at the MLK Memorial. It was time for me to rise and speak up against the injustices around me.

With everything happening all at once, none of us could have predicted the pandemic's toll on us. Many lives were lost, and it seemed there would be no end to the madness. You couldn't go outside unless necessary and had to be very cautious. A twenty-four hour day feels more like forty-eight hours when you are locked up in your home in isolation. Being unable to see friends and family started weighing on me. I didn't want to go to D.C. around my great-grandparents because I didn't want to take the chance of them getting COVID-19. You could have it and unknowingly spread the virus. They were at a higher risk of exposure because of their age. I could only have phone calls and Facetime with my loved ones. The only faces I saw every day were my mom and my dog.

Reflecting on everything I had been through, I realized I no longer wanted the world. I wanted to be in the presence of God. I knew I had an anointing and calling, but it was time to follow through. No more running. COVID-19 woke me up. Life is so precious and fleeting that the only rock I had to stand on was God. The world was shifting. I went from attending church on Sundays and seeing Broadway shows to all doors being closed. All the entertainment was over. There were no outlets for releasing tension or frustration, and I was still having to pay New York rent. I didn't know how long I could go on like that. New York didn't feel like New York. I was in a bubble of a place that used to thrive with energy and movement that now was a quiet city with nothing to do.

The effect it was having on me was different than my mom. I could weather the storm because God always provided for me, and I knew I would make it out alright. My mom, on the other hand, was struggling. Her mental health began to decline rapidly, and her bipolar schizophrenia took a toll on me. Being overworked and then isolated, she was losing her sanity. She went from hundreds of people in her face to being unable to leave the home when not working. She was having hallucinations and episodes, and I didn't know how to respond. I never had to deal with this level of my mother's health before. The pandemic seemed too much for her, and she finally reached her breaking point. It was the day she tried to kill me.

Although I was bored and wanted to have my city back the way it was, I was okay. I could deal with being home, but her, not so much. The stress of having to work that hard and deal with all those people without being on her medication was too much for her. She needed help, and every time we seemed to be drawing closer, her mental illness always tore us apart and had been affecting me since my childhood. I had to be moved from place to place because of her inefficiency to care for me and my siblings properly. It was why I stayed away as an adult. Now she was without proper medical care and medication and became too much to bear. She had become a danger to herself and others, but I didn't know it yet.

While she was off work, she had an extreme bipolar schizophrenic episode. I walked out of my bedroom late in the evening in our Brooklyn apartment and into the kitchen. I would usually do this, but this time, there was a nudge from the Holy Spirit to go check on my mom. I caught her fidgeting with the stove. The closer I got, I could see that she was trying to turn the gas on to poison us. Instead of turning it up to cook, she was just turning it so gas would seep out. She didn't notice that I was behind her when she was doing this. I quietly stepped up behind her and asked her what she was doing. Her response was something I'll never forget. She went into a fit.

She broke out into a mentally ill fury, screaming, "I was trying to kill you."

I knew what I saw, but I couldn't believe it. She began cursing at me while digging in the drawer for a knife. These kinds of episodes were nothing new to me. She was the same way when I was younger, which led me and my brothers to have to separate early in life and live with more mentally sane family members. It was different this time. I was immediately afraid because I was no longer dealing with my mom. I was in a fight with her sickness. She was supposed to be on medication so that she wouldn't have these episodes, but she always refused to take it. She didn't believe it worked. It made her sick, or whatever her excuse was for the moment. I couldn't force her to take it, so she never did. She would self-medicate instead.

I ran into my room and locked the door. I didn't know what she was capable of. She calmed down and went to bed, but I could not rest the entire night. I called my brother, uncle, and the landlord to inform them of what was happening. I told them all I was going to have to get medical care for my mom and could not live in an unsafe environment with her anymore. It wasn't all about her possibly hurting me, as she could have killed herself in the process. The landlord and I had grown closer since the death of Heather. He was outside waiting to help me, along with police and an ambulance to get her medical care. The ambulance staff coordinated getting her to a mental hospital to get the proper medication and evaluation she needed.

My mom went into a fury when they came upstairs and into our home. The emergency assistance teams could tell right away that there was some sort of mental illness. The way she was screaming and yelling wasn't normal. It was tough seeing my mom get put into an ambulance. I was the young Chantel again, wondering if she would be okay. The guilt that I had from being the one to call consumed me. Tears filled my eyes as I watched them take her away, but it was the only way she was going to get the care and assistance that she needed.

It was one of the hardest things I've ever had to do as a daughter, but I decided to make the best decision for myself. There will be a time when you have to understand your boundaries. Taking care of someone to your detriment is one of them. You don't want to die trying to save someone that you can not help. Letting go is the hardest but the best thing in certain situations. Bringing my mom there was a good idea at the time but as the world changed, so did she. I didn't know what she would do next, and I wouldn't allow her to remain and find out.

I knew that I could no longer live with my mom. There was no way I would ever be comfortable with her in my home. It took all I had to allow her to stay with me this time because I didn't want to be alone. My uncle offered a place for her to stay with him in Maryland if she agreed to take her medication regularly; otherwise, she would have to go. I loved my mother and always will, but anyone who has dealt with a family member with mental illness knows the emotional and psychological toll it can take on you. If I could have made any other choice, I would have. The last thing I wanted to see was my mom go through that, but I was already dealing with so much that I wasn't a help to her.

My mom needed more than a roof over her head. Only God could fill her void. I finally was able to rest, and the hours started flying by. A few days later, I was getting used to being alone in the apartment without her. Having a dog there kept me sane through those tough nights. I watched television often because there wasn't much to do during the pandemic. I turned to BET, and there I was. I saw myself sitting in church in the Tyler Perry movie I played in years before. I remembered recording that scene. The preacher in the film preached from Galatians 6:9, which says, "Let us not be weary in well-doing for in due season we shall reap if we faint not." As I heard those words, my spirit was tugging me. I knew my life was about to change.

While everyone around me was spiraling, I was trying to figure out which road to take. Unexpectedly, my landlord came by to visit. He was a very kind person and was coming over to check on me and see how I was doing. He was worried about me because of the recent death and situation with my mother. I let him in, and we began to talk about what had transpired with her. He let me know I wasn't to blame.

He firmly told me, "You're not a doctor, and you cannot cure your mom's mental illness. I know you love your mom, and I'm sure your mom loves you. Still, you have to make the best choice for yourself. You're not in a position to care for someone who won't take their medication. She is putting you in a situation where you could lose your life, and so could she. You've already been through enough in this apartment."

His words made so much sense to me, and I knew I made the right choice calling help for my mom. I no longer felt the extreme guilt of putting my mother out. He left, and I decided to call my friend Terry. I needed to clear out my mom's room. He helped me box up what I could and the remaining furniture I gave to my landlord.

As my life choices played out, I was reminded of what worked and what didn't. My dreams were taking off while I was with my great-grandparents. I left them to attend school and to become a big name, but that didn't happen. I ended up on the wrong side of every decision I made. Once again, I shot for the stars by moving to New York and chasing the world. I was hurt. My rap star future was mishandled, and I lived a double life trying to love God and be in the world. I needed a fresh start. Seeing myself play in *Daddy's Little Girls* showed me I've done all I could in New York. Chantel from the past was my sign to leave. I saw myself in the same trap of the enemy, surviving, and this could not be it. The rent was already astronomical in New York, and I hadn't returned to work since the hotel shut down during the pandemic. My money was dwindling.

I started researching places I wanted to stay, and Georgia caught my eye. I had little knowledge of Atlanta, but I knew it was where I should go. After seeing New Birth Church pop up on my YouTube suggestions and hearing a fiery sermon from Dr. Jamal Bryant, I realized that's where I wanted to be.

I desperately needed a new birth in my life. I met Dr. Jamal Bryant previously because he buried my stepmother during his time as a pastor in Baltimore. There was no other sign as bright as that one. Businesses, schools, and churches were still not receiving patrons nationwide, but Atlanta seemed much more open than the rest of the country. I felt God was calling me, so I applied to Hanover Buckhead Village. It was a luxury apartment building in Atlanta. I sent my information with blind faith. I didn't know what to expect, but I knew my money was running down and nothing was left for me in New York. Two days later, I got an email saying I had been approved to move in one month from that day.

Getting the yes to my apartment was the shining light that I needed. It gave me something to look forward to and a new beginning. I spent my last thirty days getting my affairs in order. I faithfully watched church services online via live streams of notable pastors like Dr. Dharius Daniels, Sarah Jakes Roberts, Pastor John F. Hannah, and Prophet Lovy—just to name a few. I knew that God would make sense of my life's mess one day. They always say that God is up to something when you're down to nothing. Those last few days proved to be what I needed to clear my head and get back on track. I chose to forgive my mother and myself. I couldn't move forward holding onto anger or unforgiveness in my heart. Time with God put me into the right mindset and perspective.

As my remaining funds declined, I had to continue to pay rent and live my last thirty days in New York. I needed to bring income home to have some money in Atlanta. I could scrape up enough money for a down payment for the apartment by selling designer items I had accumulated from my trips to Soho. I knew I would have the apartment when I got to Atlanta, but I needed to maintain it. When the end of the month came, I turned in my keys, rented a car, and drove to Atlanta with a few boxes and my dog. I had done this starting-over dance so many times. I had to leave New York behind. I had friends and support there, but I still couldn't find me. I enjoyed the New York lifestyle but was laboring at a job and not living out my calling. There had to be something better on the other side of the drive. I turned up the volume, let my hair down, and drove to the sounds of my favorite gospel songs and sermons.

Thirteen hours later, I pulled up to Hanover Buckhead Village and went into the office to pick up my keys to my new apartment, 1107. I went to the store and purchased an air mattress. I didn't have any furniture, but I only needed something to sleep on. I used all my excitement to start the job search. I saw a receptionist position within walking distance of the apartment and immediately applied for the job. I was hired on the spot. It was a psychiatrist's office called Path Group. This was the first time I had my own office. It was all working out for me. I was in a new place in life. Despite not having a car and feeling constrained to the Buckhead area, it was exactly what I needed. Not being able to attend clubs and parties forced me to spend even more time with God. I had no opportunity to get into the world to be distracted. I chose to see the best in every moment because this was my new birth. Even when my dog pierced a hole in the air mattress and I was stuck sleeping on the hardwood floor, I thanked God. I barely had anything, but what I had was enough.

I got accustomed to my new residence and remained faithful to watching church services online. No matter what, this time I trusted God. Trusting him always paid off. One day while I was walking my dog, I was followed by a man. It was early in the morning, and he was in a Range Rover. I had brushed him off as being a creep. This was the same thing that happened in Los Angeles, and I was more attentive this time. Looking back at that particular situation makes me think of Hebrews 13:2: "Be not forgetful to entertain strangers; for thereby some have entertained angels unaware." After almost ten minutes of following me around, I continued to brush him off.

Finally, he spoke and said, "Hey, you never know who God is sending to help you."

The alarms inside of me began to ring, but I had a calmness that he was okay. Mr. Stephen and I exchanged numbers, and he left. He called me later that day, and I mentioned that I had just moved to Atlanta.

As soon as I said that, he randomly asked, "Do you have any furniture?"

I replied, "No."

He said, "Look, God is telling me to help you. I have a storage unit with brand-new furniture from Modani Furniture. I will deliver it to your building tomorrow."

I truly didn't believe him and honestly was used to liars and the disappointment of things seeming too good to be true. In my mind, I thought this guy would want something. I hoped he didn't think I was going to sleep with him or anything. He could have his furniture because I'm not that kind of woman. I was completely wrong and blown away. The employee at the apartment complex front desk called me the next day, saying there were two movers downstairs with furniture. I cried. He was telling the truth. I could see how God could use anyone to bless you. Everyone wasn't scum or manipulative. God set people aside to help me when I sought Him instead of the nightlife. I sat in awe as the movers brought in a beautiful table, couch, bed, and TV. It was like one of those miraculous moments in the Bible where God provided water, manna, and quail. It was fantastic to see the hand of God at work. I went from sleeping on the floor in Buckhead to a fully furnished apartment overnight.

A warm bed after sleeping on the floor solidified this was the place I was supposed to be. I followed God correctly, and He provided for me. These are the things I no longer take for granted. You look at every blessing differently when you've been homeless, hungry, or had to sleep on a floor. Saying thank you for a roof over your head and clothes on your back becomes more than just something you picked up in church. When you go through a storm, the shine of the sun's rays and the color of the rainbow hit differently.

Now that I had furniture to check off my list, I still needed a car. I wasn't too pressed about it because I was within walking distance of work and home. Once I started trying, I was met with challenge after challenge trying to get a license in Atlanta. The first was needing a registered driver and car in Georgia for a driver's test. I only knew one person before moving to Atlanta, the producer from Los Angeles. We had a falling out because he demanded $20,000 per song that he made for me; otherwise, I wouldn't have the rights to them. He also made several sexual advances, even going as far as groping me. I realized he was not the person I thought he was when meeting him early on. He showed me that no matter what, I had to trust God for what I needed. I trusted that God would send the right people into my life, just like Mr. Stephen. I would keep my heart posture toward God, bed, car, or nothing at all. God still deserved all the praise because I was still alive despite all the attempts of the enemy to kill and destroy me.

The months quickly passed in Buckhead, and I found myself on New Year's Eve at the end of 2020. As I ushered in the new year in Atlanta, I was getting my life back together while the world was separated and isolated. I could have died at the hands of COVID-19 or my mother. I had to wear a mask and protest in the streets for the deaths of people in my culture. Somehow, God picked me up and placed me in Buckhead, Atlanta. I was so grateful. I celebrated the start of 2021 by tuning into New Birth's New Year's Eve service online. I turned my living room into a full-blown praise and worship area. I praised God through song and words. I thanked Him for how far He brought me and for never leaving me. I didn't know what 2021 would have in store, but I fully trusted God.

CHAPTER 9

Silent Rain

WHEN YOU DON'T SEE THE STORM COMING, YOU ARE LEFT UNPREPARED.

— Chantel Dean

I TRULY BELIEVE GOD SENDS ANGELS AND HELPERS in times of need. God can use anyone to bless you, and they will not always look like you. That's the attitude that led to my next miracle of getting my own car again. I was getting around the best way I knew how by walking. After years of not having a valid driver's license let alone a decent car, I met a burn survivor named Trip. We were at a place called The Battery when we sparked up a conversation. Ultimately, he let me—a total stranger—use his car for my driver's test in Marietta. I can't tell you what I said or what he saw in me, but I knew it was God. I scheduled an appointment at the DMV and went to take my driver's license test. I walked in with confidence and walked out with a driver's license for the first time in almost eight years. It was on paper until my real one would arrive by mail.

Giddy, I was ready for a car. I was working and learning from my mistakes in the past of not saving. I put money away for a rainy day and saved enough for a down payment. I had my eye on a used white BMW, and I could not believe it when I was able to purchase it. I handed over the money and drove off in my dream car. It seemed like life was finally coming together for the first time in a long time. I was where I was supposed to be, and everything lined up for me. I kept my eyes on the cross all this time, but I changed my focus once I got to my car. I decided I wanted to go out and see what Atlanta was all about. I didn't know the city and places that were shut down due to COVID-19 were beginning to open back up. I had FOMO (Fear of missing out) from months of sitting in the house. I started thinking with a worldly mindset and craving to see what nightlife looked like. I heard about it, but I wanted to experience it myself.

It's a shame how quickly we forget about God once He gives us what we want. I was easily distracted as soon as I received a gift from Him. He taught me the wisdom to save to get a car, and instead of going to the church I moved to Georgia to attend, I found myself in the clubs. It was so easy to get off track because I had access to go places. I went from reading my Bible daily to being on nightclub flyers overnight. God never calls the qualified. He qualifies the called, but the Atlanta scene was seductive. My calling from God to preach became a burden to me. I didn't want to sit inside and read the word. I could make money promoting the nightclubs of Atlanta. I could party, drink, and have a good time. I needed to relieve stress after the situations I had been through. I wanted the life I was living. It was exciting, and every night had different levels of fun. I wanted to be a typical thirty-one year-old woman who could attend events and not feel the pressure of leading people to God, so I became her. I began reneging on all my promises to God. I completely stopped reading my word. I no longer went to church online or in person. Sunday was now for Saturday night recovery, not church services. How quickly I had fallen! God has a way of letting you know you are wrong.

In the Old Testament, He sent Moses and Joshua to ensure the children of Israel kept the covenant with Him after He brought them out. God wants us to do right, but we choose wrong. It's our sinful nature, but He loves us enough to get or send someone to shake us up. He came to get me in such a masterful way. I went out with a friend of a friend one night to party. We had a great time, but they needed a ride back to Douglasville because they had been drinking. I didn't mind, and we took off and headed for their place. I went from 30 mph to 55 mph in a 45 mph zone in a few seconds. It was at that moment I found myself surrounded by three white cops. I knew exactly why I was pulled over. They had a right, too, because I was speeding. I had not been drinking.

Let me tell you how God works. The police officer handcuffed me and put me in the patrol car. The person that was with me continued to stay in the car. I was on my way to jail that night on speeding charges. It was the wake-up call I needed.

God gently nudged me to say, "Chantel, you're going the wrong way."

God and I always had a daddy-daughter relationship. I was the child who would get the most severe punishment for getting off-track simply because I knew better. He always seemed to wake me spiritually whenever I fell off my walk. My mugshot was taken, and I was charged with speeding. I would later be able to get the charges dismissed, but I shouldn't have been out of the apartment. The Holy Spirit told me to stay home, and I disobeyed. As I stated earlier, I was reneging on God.

I was released shortly after at 6 a.m. I walked over to a Douglasville gas station and stood outside. I pulled out my phone to dial the person who'd driven off in my car after being arrested, only to get no answer. Standing there, I felt so used and broken. He wasn't a friend to me or cared about my well-being. I was arrested driving him home. I was getting anxious because I needed to go home and had no clue what to do. I was new to Atlanta and didn't know anyone. Suddenly, two young Black men approached me.

They asked. "Are you okay, Miss?"

Their kindness shattered me, and crying was my default. They backed up a little to give me room and let me know they were only there to assist. I told them what I experienced, and they listened and consoled me.

I genuinely believe they were angels sent to help me. They offered to take me to get my car, and I agreed to ride with them. They seemed trustworthy, so I directed them to the person's home. They drove me to his house where my car sat in the driveway. I got out and knocked on the door but to my surprise, it was open. I walked inside, grabbed my keys, and vowed never to go to Douglasville again. I thanked the men who brought me and left. I cried the entire ride back from Douglasville to Buckhead, listening to Marvin Sapp's "Never Would Have Made It." This was my last and final straw with myself. I could not keep having God save me to keep leaving Him. All the crying and praying I did to have my life turned around, He did it. He kept his word to me, but I threw away my part of the agreement every time I saw a sparkle of what I wanted. It was no longer about me. It was time to be about God.

I got home, washed my face, and lie down. I couldn't believe that I was arrested, but I thanked God there wasn't any alcohol in my system. Instead of being home, I could have had a DUI or DWI. God brought me out, but the question I had to ask myself was why did I keep going in? I made myself stay in the house and went through a bit of depression and isolation the following months of May until the start of August 2021. I only left my Buckhead apartment for necessities and not leisure. I wanted to avoid trouble and situations that didn't fit my calling. I no longer wanted to disappoint God or myself.

At the beginning of September 2021, I strongly wanted to return to D.C. and spend time with my great-grandparents. It was a gut feeling, and I knew it was God telling me I needed to return home. I requested time off and took a two-week vacation back home. I wanted to spend time with them because I missed them. My great-grandpa was ninty-nine years old, still lively and preaching. My great-grandma was also up in age and in her 90s. I boarded the plane in Atlanta with gratitude for God keeping them alive and well. There was such an expectation in my spirit for them. As soon as I got off the plane, I received a call from my Aunt Milini who frequently checked on them.

"Hey, Chantel, I have to tell you something," she said.

"Sure, what is it?"

"Chantel, your great-grandmother fell down the stairs," she said.

"Is she okay?" I asked.

"Yes."

"Okay, thank God. I just landed, and I'm on my way."

I thanked God she hadn't broken anything, but she was seriously hurting. It seemed the timing of my return was divine, and I did all I could to help. She was placed in a nursing home around the corner for most of the two weeks I was home. They were able to take great care of her and attend to all of her needs. I went to check on her daily. I felt that this was why God told me to go home, so I could be with her and check her well-being. Due to her absence, I had more time with my great-grandfather.

One day, a strong presence came over me when I walked into the house. I felt in my heart this would be the last time I would be around my great-grandfather. I couldn't shake it. It didn't seem real because although he was ninty-nine, he was so vibrant and full of life. I acted as though it wasn't true, and for two weeks, I did whatever I could to help out. I brought food home daily, took out the trash, cleaned the house, and spent quality time with the only father I'd genuinely had. He had patience and a subtle greatness about him that mirrored the love of God. Nearly a week and a couple of days later, my great-grandmother returned.

For years I'd heard him yell, "Ruthie!" from the bottom of the staircase to the top.

She would always yell back, "Dave!" from the top of the stairs down to where he was. They would communicate in this cute way whenever someone called the house phone for either of them. Having her back home and hearing the familiar sounds of their voices warmed my heart. Then, I would sit with my great-grandpa all day. These were the priceless moments I craved no matter where I lived.

At home, I often sat in my great-grandpa's home office in his Lazy Boy chair. It brought me closer to him. I was overwhelmed with tears as the gospel song "Grateful" by Hezekiah Walker began to resound through the speakers from Google Play. During the pandemic, I set up the system so my great-grandparents could listen to music on demand. My great-grandfather loved to stay up to date on the newest technology. He was sitting there and heard my sobbing but didn't address it. What did he know that I didn't?

I reflected on my life and how my great-grandparents had always been the only people in my corner. They never judged me and ensured I had food and wouldn't starve. They had always been my parents, and they showed me love. It was remarkable. There I was, sitting, watching him fall asleep. I knew my great-grandparents couldn't live forever, but I wanted them to. I wasn't ready for them to leave me. It was in that instant, sitting behind him with silent tears as he slept in his favorite chair, that I realized again that this was going to be the last time I would see him alive. I took a deep breath and soaked in the last moments I would have with my great-grandfather. There was no sickness, no signs that anything was wrong. The Holy Spirit was internally preparing me to be strong when the time came.

My great-grandma came into the room and told me she needed help climbing the stairs. I walked her up and settled her in their bedroom. It brought me peace whenever I could do anything for them after all they had done for me. I promptly returned to the office with my great-grandfather to see if he was awake, but he was still sleeping in his chair. I sat back down and gazed at him. I felt tremendous gratitude and joy for God bringing him through the storm. My mind went to scripture, and I recalled the verse, "When my father and my mother forsake me, then the Lord will take me up" (Psalm 27:10). Not only did the Lord take me up, but he also gave me phenomenal great-grandparents. They instilled in me a love for scripture and our Heavenly Father. They also taught me great character, morals, values, and the importance of forgiveness and resilience. I basked in the thoughtfulness of my great-grandparents to not only take me in when I was younger but take care of me. I stayed there in that spot until the sun went down. I could smell my great-grandfather's Lagerfeld fragrance and his scent in the room. All the while, words were not said between us, but our silence spoke volumes.

I found myself going upstairs to rest in the room I grew up in, reminiscing about how this home had always been my refuge. The creaky stairs, chipped paint, smells, and wallpaper made this house a home. It wasn't a brand-new modern apartment that made a house a home. It was the love given to you through the people living there. I continued to help my great-grandparents for the last few days before returning to Atlanta. My vacation was up, and I had to return to work to maintain my stability there. My great-grandma needed my help, and I fought myself to go. Being able to help her around the house and to cook for her were the things that I enjoyed. I wanted them to have no worries that someone would be there for them, but I had to leave.

The day I was set to go, I told my great-grandpa, "I'm moving back here."

I knew it wasn't me speaking but God speaking through me. In my carnal mind, I had a fully furnished apartment and car in Atlanta. I also had a job and income. I would come back to nothing again, and I didn't want that. I wanted to be able to help with tangible assets. I soon realized God had a bigger plan for me, and He had given me spiritual insight into the future. I had all I would need at my great-grandparent's home because God was there. With him, I would have provisions and income would follow. I thought I knew God, but He always let me know man can never understand the magnitude of God. Material things were replaceable. God tested me on that several times, and I failed the open-book test.

A few days later, after returning to Atlanta, I got a late-night call from my Aunt Milini. She was the granddaughter and primary caretaker of my great-grandparents. Aunt Milini is also one of the most selfless people ever known. As soon as I answered, I knew something wasn't right. One, she never called me late, and two, the raspiness of her voice let me know she had been crying.

I asked her what happened, and she said, "Grandpa died today."

Even as I retell my story, I'm so emotional because to know him was to love him. He was a fantastic father, pastor, leader, and friend. I went to Los Angeles, New York, and Atlanta, chasing the illusion of fame and fortune. Everything God had called me to do was already inside me, but I had spent so many years running away from it. My great-grandpa had been the one to license me to preach, and I was so glad he could see me stand in the pulpit and give a sermon before he passed away. I hung up the phone and spent the rest of the night crying. I wanted to see him and hear his voice again, so I frantically went to YouTube. I played sermons he preached at the church, which were uploaded from Sunday services. I stood up and looked around my apartment. I finally had furniture and a car. Now nothing I accumulated even mattered. It was worthless to me. I left my great-grandparents to return to this lonely place to work and still not do what God called me to do. Enough was enough.

I packed whatever I could in my car for my trip back to D.C. I decided to go back and help be a caretaker for my great-grandmother. I didn't care about the apartment or the job anymore. I wanted to finally be there for the woman who was always there for me in my time of need. I knocked on my neighbor's door and told him I had to leave in the morning. I left my keys with him because I only had three more months on my lease, and I would not be returning. I had been trying to break my lease, but the apartment complex gave me a hard time. It was the post-pandemic era, but getting tenants with jobs was difficult. A lot of people lost their income and were not able to pay rent. The apartment management was trying to hold tight to those who could afford to pay them. I didn't have time to put out that fire. I needed to go, so I agreed to pay the rent for three more months. I didn't care that I wouldn't be living there. My neighbor assured me he would take care of the furniture and even gave me cash for the items I was leaving behind.

The next day, I got up early to drive the eleven hours to D.C. It was interesting because there was a cloud in the shape of a cross nearly the entire ride. God was with me. The sun started to go down in the sky, but I kept driving until I got in front of my great-grandparents' house. I pulled up as I had done many times over the years. I cut off the ignition, and it hit me. This was the first time I would walk into the house and not see my great-grandfather. The emotions I held onto so tightly on the road burst out of me. I cried as hard and long as I could in the car so I could be there for my great-grandma when I saw her. I cleaned myself up but didn't have the energy to get anything out of my car. The drive itself had taken so much out of me. Finally, I walked up the path to the door, put in my key, and turned the knob to the only place I ever knew to be my true home.

I opened the door as me, but I walked in as a full-time caretaker to my great-grandma. I wanted to make sure she was okay—she was losing her husband, our church was losing its pastor, the city lost an angel, and I lost my father. The first few steps into the house, I saw my great-grandma sitting in her Lazy Boy chair, which always sat opposite my great-grandfather's. They were only separated by the front door decorated with a mirrored cross. They always had their two chairs on each side of each other. I tried my best to hide my pain and not show anyone how deeply I was torn that he was gone. I felt I had to be a sign of strength when I entered the house.

I glanced over at his chair. I knew he wasn't there, but I'd been used to seeing him sit there my whole life. He would mostly watch the Word Network and occasionally Westerns. It was natural for me to look there, but it was a harsh reality. He wouldn't be there anymore. Before I broke, I held it together and walked over to my great-grandma. She was sitting there so strong, even though I knew that without assistance, she couldn't even get back upstairs. All I could do was hug her. I held on so tightly to her to feel him one more time because I couldn't imagine losing her, too. I finally got up and went to sit in his blue Lazy Boy chair. My great-grandmother and I exchanged no words for an hour. I had no words to say. It felt like right before I left and he was there sleeping in his chair in silence. The entire house felt empty without his presence. I lost one of the most influential people in my life, and there was nothing anyone could do.

My great-grandma was ready for bed, and I helped her climb the stairs. I went outside to my car and got my suitcase. I went to my bedroom to unpack and sat on the end of the bed. I remember watching my great-grandpa come in every morning to get his clothes out because we shared a closet when I was growing up. So many small details came back to me that I would miss. I tossed and turned. I kept trying to find my way to sleep but was wide awake. I sat there and cried. I was grieving him, and I needed to. I stayed up that night, not knowing what I was doing with my life. I left my entire apartment in Atlanta and my job on the spot. Was I crazy?

I left Georgia Friday morning and had all intentions of attending church on Sunday. I pictured how hard it would be to walk into the church where we'd shared memories—the challenge of being in the place where I was baptized. I taught and preached my first sermon there. Being there would be tough because my great-grandfather was not only a father to me but also my pastor and spiritual leader. His presence wasn't only in this home but also in the church. I couldn't imagine walking in there and not seeing him sitting in the pulpit preaching, in his office ready to counsel others, or preparing to give of himself. He was in every aspect of my spiritual, physical, and mental upbringing. No matter where I went, part of me would miss seeing him there.

Saturday was spent organizing, cleaning, and caring for my great-grandmother. Sunday morning came and I drove up to the church. The air seemed thinner. My great-grandparents' protection and prayers had sheltered me from the many storms of life. Many of those prayers were birthed in the church I was staring at. I pressed my way past the ushers and into the doors. It was as I remembered with its red seats, red carpeted floors, and beautiful stained glass windows. I walked forward, and I could feel many people watching me to see if I would fold and if I needed help. They were grieving with me, not just for me. My great-grandfather impacted not only me but the entire community. To that point, he would have a street named after him in D.C. adjacent to the church.

The service preached by Rev. Omar Buchanan, an associate minister, was emotional, but I made it through. I gathered my things and was headed for the door as soon as service ended. Despite my haste to leave, I wasn't quick enough. The deacons flagged me down and pulled me to the side.

I heard, "Reverend Chantel Dean."

It was a title that held a weight I had yet to live up to and at times, didn't know if I deserved.

"We want you to start preaching some Sundays in place of your great-grandfather."

I couldn't hold my tears when they said that to me. It was God saying that I couldn't run anymore. I was face to face with my calling. It was, as the scripture states, the choice of whom you will serve this day

(Joshua 24:15). I chose God. There was no better way to honor God than through my obedience to Him. My yes made it real.

This was a serious task to shepherd a congregation.

I said, "Now I must prepare a sermon and remain in the word of God."

CHAPTER 10

After the Storm

RENEWAL AND RESTORATION ARE HERE.
— Chantel Dean

INTERESTINGLY, AFTER HIS PASSING, MY GREAT-grandpa would show up paranormally in the house to let me know his spirit was around. There were nights when I would sit on the couch after feeling sad or burnt out, and the television would turn on. Cutting on by itself, I would see Jimmy Swaggart on a channel he watched often or one of his other favorite gospel networks. I would smile because I knew it was him. I needed to keep the word in my heart to make me feel better and lift my spirits. I would often sit and laugh when he made his presence known. My great-grandma was the opposite. If it happened when she was around, it would freak her out.

As I sat one night on the porch, I saw him fly in the sky with angel wings over me. It was what I needed at the time to know that he was okay. Days passed by, and I would watch as my great-grandmother slept in her rocking chair, thinking about how she and my great-grandfather did their best to keep me close to the Lord. Staring at her, I felt multiple emotions. Grief is such a tricky thing to navigate. I was becoming okay with my great-grandfather being gone, but I knew my great-grandmother would also leave this earth sooner than later. Her health was declining. I was at peace with it because my great-grandparents planted seeds for the storm's weather inside me since I was a child. They were my anchors on earth. They raised me despite the flaws of my parents. I worked so hard so they could see that every sacrifice they made paid off. It had been exactly fourteen years since I lived in their house as a teenager with big dreams and high hopes of becoming a movie star. It was clear that God always had a purpose and a plan for my life, and that journey always included them.

The people who hurt me made me stronger. The ones who turned their back on me allowed God to show off who He was as my Father. I was no longer the naive seventeen year old moving to Hollywood. I was a grown woman with more wisdom, experience, and faith in God. Although it hurt losing my great-grandfather, I knew he was in a much better place. He had a "Well done" from God, but I didn't, yet. God wanted more from me, and my story had to be told. I couldn't die with it inside of me. It was time for me to fully become who God called me to be.

Sunday was coming, and I would be preaching for the first time in a long time. I needed to write my first sermon to fill my role as Reverend Chantel Dean. As I studied to find a topic, my inspiration came from an unlikely source. A man named Gregory called our home for as long as I could remember.

The phone would ring multiple times throughout the day just for him to say, "Don't worry, be happy!"

He had special needs due to a disability and always came to Mount Zion with a joyful attitude and a message. One thing about Gregory, he never missed a day calling the house. I genuinely believe that Gregory was an angel sent to remind us to be truly happy.

The Bible clearly states in Philippians 4:6, "Don't worry about anything; instead, pray about everything. Tell God what you need, and thank him for all he has done." The confirmation that I made the right decision to preach came when I walked into the house after church. I was about to tell my great-grandmother the excellent news. I was going to start preaching again.

Before I could, the phone rang. My great-grandma said, "That's probably Gregory."

I picked up the phone and said, "Hello, this is the Davis residence."

All I heard was, "Don't worry, be happy," and he said it so confidently. He knew it was me and responded, "You were in L.A., and you were here, and you were there."

I told him, "Yeah, I've been to all those places, Gregory."

He finally said, "I just want to tell you, don't worry, be happy."

The title of my message became: "Don't worry, be happy."

After preaching that sermon, I began to feel more comfortable behind the pulpit. My nervousness subsided the more I answered the call. My following sermon would officially be my third time in the pulpit, which my great-grandfather graced for so many years. It was the message I needed the most. I thought God had given the word to the congregation, but it was actually for me. Becoming a full-time caretaker for my great-grandmother, even with Aunt Milini's help, was a job. It is an undertaking, and I didn't understand the capacity needed for the task. There were plenty of instances where I experienced caretaker fatigue. I became overwhelmed by my daily responsibilities. My great-grandmother sometimes had accidents when she couldn't make it to the bathroom. I would have to clean up and change her. She also needed help climbing the stairs, so I had to take her.

I bit my tongue and kept my woes to myself. It seemed petty to complain. The problem was I had already done this dance back in high school. At that time, her daughter and my grandmother, Lanie, was dying of melanoma. I would help change her bandages and clean up her accidents while making the distinguished honor roll list at school. It was to the point that whenever I would hear a noise, I'd jump up to see if she was okay. It caused me to have a type of PTSD. Dealing with my great-grandmother brought back those memories of the sixteen-year-old me—the girl trying to balance school and caring for others. I would lay in bed crying at night because there was nothing I could do to stop the melanoma from eating away at my mother figure. My great-grandmother was a two-time breast cancer survivor, but her daughter, my grandmother, was not. She fought a long battle with melanoma but lost on June 18, 2007.

She passed days after the news of my stepmother's suicide. Michelle, my stepmother, left a rose on her desk at work before ultimately driving to Solomon's Island. This was a Maryland community where she and my father shared a second home outside of Baltimore.

She wrote a suicide note and swallowed multiple pills that day. My father was the one to find her in their bed. This all happened the year before I would leave for college in California.

I started feeling guilty for wanting to take a break and having caretaker burnout. She had done so much for me. How could I not be there for her? I could never fill my great-grandfather's role or take his place, but I wanted to be what she no longer had. As people, we're not always honest about the fact that caregiver burnout is a common occurrence. I had become physically, emotionally, mentally, and financially exhausted. I planned to be there for her the best that I could. I prepared her breakfast, lunch, and dinner, ensuring she always ate despite the fact there wasn't much money. My great-grandpa had spent their money and his time pouring into the church, community, and other people while he was living. He was such a giver, but it was a struggle sometimes without that income and the little my great-grandmother received. I was grateful I could provide for her and ensure she didn't miss any meals. We couldn't afford a nursing home, and my great-grandmother made it clear she didn't want to go even if we could.

For the next three months, I continued to pay my rent in Atlanta until my lease ended while living in D.C. My neighbor did as he promised and handled everything for me. He had all the furniture removed and turned in my keys for me. Since I didn't have to return to do those things, I spent every day with my great-grandma. We were talking and laughing, and she became my new best friend. There were moments where I sat in my great-grandpa's office and grinned from ear to ear. God allowed me to take care of my great-grandma because, in essence, she took care of me. This was now my opportunity to return the favor. Supporting my great-grandmother was humbling, and I acknowledged all the sacrifices my great-grandparents made for me.

Although there were great days, there were also moments of immense guilt. I would worry whenever I left her home alone. I recall going to the grocery store and my great-grandma fell while she was in the kitchen. Her cell phone was in her pocket, and she was able to call my Aunt Milini, who in turn called me. I rushed over and was able to get her off the ground. Those days made me think. As much as I would like to say I was ready to give up my life to serve my great-grandmother, I wasn't. My burnout turned into inner resentment of everyone around me in their thirties with the freedom to live as they chose. People my age were at the stage of life where they were getting married and having children, while I was still living out of a suitcase in my great-grandparents' house. My peers were buying homes and into their careers. I craved to have stability, but my life was always in a constant storm, ever-changing, and always moving. I wondered if a rainbow would ever come for me.

My unhappiness grew intensely and was a feeling I felt all too often. It symbolized the push into the next chapter of who I was becoming. I was stagnant for too long. My time in D.C. was coming to a close, and I felt like a plant outgrowing my container. God's voice was a tiny whisper, which seemed to be pulling me back to Atlanta. I no longer feared starting over because caretaking had become a storm of its own. I had to make these latter years of life on earth work.

In an audible voice, I heard God say, "It's time."

After nearly one year and six months, I was ready to leave. I packed up my bags and filled up my trunk with the same possessions I brought to my great-grandparents' home to return back to Atlanta. God told me where to go but no other directions. I was in the position to trust Him, and I would have to take the first step so the next one could appear.

I finished what I came to D.C. for, which was to preach and be the shoulder for my great-grandmother. I helped our church in one of its toughest seasons of transition. What was required of me was completed, and I needed to move on. God even provided new caretakers to solidify my exit and cover my absence with my great-grandmother. God had given me a day to leave, and it had finally arrived. I awoke to begin my move back to Atlanta at 5 a.m. There was something waiting for me, and I wanted to find out what. God gifted me wisdom, and it was time to use it. As I walked around the house to take one last glance, I looked at photos of a younger me hanging on the walls with a smile. I would never forget where I came from. It was up to me to find that version of Chantel again. The version before the world told me what I should be. I wanted to be that person who gets back up when she falls and decides to dream bigger each day. When a child says their future career, no one shoots them down. It's only when we mature that people tend to redefine us. Then we try to fit into the mold they created for us. That's when God steps in to remind us of who we are.

Preparing to leave, I thought of God and how He had worked throughout my life. Once you begin on the path of your purpose with God, He has a way of telling you something that doesn't seem logical or make sense. God told Noah to build an ark, something that had never been created, based on God's measurements and materials. Noah had to prepare for flood waters when there had never even been rain. God gives us all what we need if we have an ear to hear Him and trust His word when He instructs us. God will never put anyone in the middle of a storm without a safety net or a life vest. When the storm gets bad and you wonder why God put you there, you must remain patient and vigilant to stand on God's word. We must be open to an all-knowing God because He has our best interest at heart. He will put us in the right place at the right time to meet the right people. We have to be open and obedient to move forward and stay in position.

Even with all God teaches us, we continue to make mistakes. The positive side is that mistakes grow us. We rebuild ourselves through every storm because we learned something. Some storms bring drizzles of rain, while others are thunderstorms. However they start, know that the sun must come out at the end. Life may not have turned out the way I pictured it, but it turned out perfect for who I needed to be, what I needed to learn, and how I needed to grow. A flower cannot blossom without water, nor can you become who you're meant to be without storms.

The eleven hours back to Atlanta were full of what I was supposed to do. Guided by God, I drove my car through the Southern states. After stopping at a rest area in North Carolina, I noticed a cop following me onto the highway. Not soon after, he pulled me over. I didn't know what would happen but knew to remain calm because I had done nothing wrong. He came to the car, and I rolled my window down slightly.

"Good afternoon, young lady. What do you do for a

living? This car is way too nice for you. Are you some kind of hip-hop person or something?"

Huh? There was no reason for him to ask me that. He didn't start with an explanation of why he pulled me over. If he had given me a ticket, it would have been a lie.

I said, "I am a minister." He stumbled over his next words when I asked, "Why did you pull me over?"

He stood over my window and said, "Oh, well I see nothing here. You can go." He let me go, knowing he had no reason to pull me over.

I knew it was all a test. I would not let it discourage me as I was nearing South Carolina and continued to drive. It would be a few more hours until I reached my final destination in Atlanta. I had given everything I had away. There was no high rise in Buckhead waiting for me anymore. I would have to pull my resources and find another job. To most, my decision to leave D.C. seemed illogical. I was comfortable in D.C. I had a roof over my head, a car, and my family. God has a way to make you comfortably uncomfortable. He did not call me to be comfortable there. Instead, I was called to save souls. I was back home to enhance my gift in a known environment where it could flourish under the right atmosphere. God set my life up in a way that would pull the best out of me.

Getting to Atlanta, my new living circumstances

were challenging. I was no longer trying to live fancy on the outside while lacking on the inside of my home. I was on a mission and was being called into isolation. Elevation requires separation. I repositioned myself because quitting was not an option. This time, I found a room in a home in Southwest, and it was just right for me. Though the neighborhood I was staying in was not the best, I knew my protection came from God. Where I had lived previously, I had a washer and dryer, but not in my new place. I would regularly make trips to the laundromat where I would socialize and meet new people. I would question what God was really up to. I would be lying if I didn't say fully committing to God can sometimes be challenging. Everything He takes us through is for a reason. I went from living a luxurious life to being a caretaker to living in one room without amenities. What I knew about God was that He would let me go in the fire but not let me burn. He would let me go in the water but not let me drown.

Many of us are rebellious to God. We turn away from God after we get what we want and then cry out to Him to help us out of what we got ourselves into. I am thankful God didn't let me die in my wilderness. I continued to commit myself to Christ more than ever and built a relationship with Him in Georgia. I needed to be fed and have fellowship with other Christians, so I began to attend church regularly. I felt at home and met more people. I wanted to serve and be the hands and feet of Jesus. As my networking grew, I was around more influential people who knew the word and were excellent teachers of it. I became a student under some of Atlanta's most dynamic preachers. I was getting my feet wet in the gospel of Jesus Christ and applied to attend seminary. I was accepted and began taking diverse leadership classes at Spelman College. I decided not to let anything distract me from God. I was going to be obedient. I stayed out of the clubs and far away from the nightlife. I no longer wanted the taste of liquor. My soul was only thirsty for God night and day.

When I moved back to Atlanta, I still had some funds available. That's how I got a place to stay, but I needed to work. I applied to several places due to my experience as a front desk hotel worker and a medical receptionist. Eventually, I got a job at a pain management clinic. There, I became an undercover prayer warrior. The light of Christ began to shine on me the more I spent time with God. It didn't take long before I was offered a better position at a medical clinic working with patients who had HIV. Matthew 25:23 says, "His master replied, 'Well done, good and faithful servant! You have been faithful with a few things; I will put you in charge of many things." I knew my elevation was directly tied to paying my tithes faithfully and praying for others. I truly believe God can cure the incurable.

My life was turning around, and I could see doors opening for me. Then my phone rang, it was Aunt Milini.

"Chantel, grandma is gone."

My great-grandma passed away at the age of ninty-nine. She was all I had left. I immediately went to the closet of my job and cried hysterically. I didn't know what to do, say, or how to feel. My great-grandmother was an amazing woman of God. I knew this day would come, but I was dreading it. I took solace in knowing she had seen me stand in my calling and was proud her prayers had paid off. Every morning since I could remember, I watched my great-grandmother kneel at the side of her bed and pray for hours. I could only imagine the number of times my name was mentioned in those prayers and how her very prayers saved me day after day, year after year. She taught me how to pray and talk to God. In that instant, I knew the mantle was passed to me to step up as the prayer warrior of the family. It would take an immense amount of maturity as family can sometimes be the ones that hurt you the most. I began praying and worshiping like never before, right there in my work closet.

Several epiphanies occurred to me following my great-grandmother's death. Not only did I have to swallow the reality of not hearing her voice and her laugh, but we would be losing my childhood home. Losing the house hurt my heart as I realized the next time I'd step foot in, it would also be my last. I once again took a leave of absence from work to return home. I arrived in D.C. late in the evening at our home. I would no longer have a backup house. My safety net would be gone. God was letting me know my past was over, and I had to steer into the future. I took a deep breath and walked on the patio. It was where I would sit and hold riveting conversations with the most important people in my life. I continued to the door, but there was no reason to knock because no one would answer. I used my key one last time. I was approached by the faint fragrance of her perfume throughout the room. The key opened a gateway to a museum of memories and photos. I teared up and touched anything along the way, a pillow they used or a blanket left downstairs. My great-grandfather's office was my breaking point. I burst into tears at the thought they were both gone before finally making my way upstairs.

Once I reached the top of the stairs, one creak at a time, I entered my great-grandparents' bedroom. It was still the same as if they'd walk in any minute. I reminisced on the days I would sleep on a cot next to their bed because I was scared of the dark. I laughed at the memories of laying out my church dress and rehearsing the scripture I would say weekly at Sunday School when it was my turn to stand up. I found myself at the edge of the bed with my great-grandfather's Lagerfeld cologne. I sprayed the last little bit in the air to smell him one more time. Briefly, I was comforted.

The funeral was the next day, but the hours of the night moved slowly. I walked around the entire house, taking in every detail. The floorboards, the paint choice on the walls, the pots and pans she cooked with. Everything was a memory in time. Photographs taken before I was thought about told the stories of their lives. Ruth Burns from Burnsville, North Carolina, met John Davis from Ghent, Kentucky. Much later came my life, which was full of storms yet still so full of purpose. You can never know where you're going until you know where you've come from. My very humble beginnings shaped me as a person and a preacher. I could see the God of my great-grandparents with my own eyes, and I'd come to know Him for myself. I could choose to dance in the rain or drown in the flood. Through every storm, I knew many more smiles were waiting to take place at the end.

CONCLUSION

The Rainbow

"The storm did not come to kill you. It came to reposition you!" Those words rang in my head as I pondered where life had brought me to that point. Every storm must end, and the storms that came into my life were never meant to break me but to build my faith. After the journeys I had experienced, there were so many hidden gems for me to share and pass along to you, the reader.

Always remember sunny days bring warmth, growth, and comfort. While the sun shines, bask in its radiance because the rain is coming. Rainy days aren't meant to bring you down. They bring nutrients, strength, and courage. When the rain shifts to an unavoidable storm, realize God is your shelter. He will send friends to hold your umbrella. The storms in our lives may get complicated, but they were never intended to wash us away. They push us into our destined place.

I searched for the specific version of myself that fame and fortune would bring. I didn't know that each place would have its own lessons, mistakes, and trials. Each pulled out a new part of me. I was developing faith and wisdom in God, which would change my life. Going to Los Angeles, I found the "naive" version of me—the young, green girl in the big city who trusted every stranger and was too prideful to leave. I stayed there too long trying to prove my plan to be on the big screen as the next actress. I had to be in California. Big names came from there, and I pressed my way to stay. I was in a horrible relationship and had a terrible roommate. The glimmer of hope was the good Samaritans I met in between who allowed me to sleep on their couch and vent to them. I was homeless and still wouldn't leave. Do you believe that? God had to teach me He was my provider and would lead me. When people failed me and I wanted to give up on life, God showed me that all things are possible with Him, not man.

After getting a reset back in D.C., I went to New York. My passion for fame followed me there, too. I saw the bright lights of Broadway. My drive led me down a musical career path. This was the "I am grown" version of Chantel. I had friends and support in the Big Apple, a job, and an apartment. I lost myself in the music industry and sight of who God is. Thankfully, I found Him again right before losing my roommate, dealing with a pandemic, and confronting my mother's mental health issues. He was my comfort through it all. Finally getting my footing with God, I went to Atlanta. I craved to have fancy things. Let's say I had high-class taste. There is nothing wrong with wanting those things. You should have things. They just shouldn't have you. This was the "wherever the wind blows" version of Chantel.

I had a white BMW, a penthouse apartment, and a nice income. Excited to attend church and grow closer to God was Atlanta's purpose, but I presented myself as a party girl. I was free and wild. I finally had it all: a social life. I had the opportunity to enjoy what the city had to offer. I had privacy in my home and could hide what I was doing. People only knew what I told them. My free will left me literally arrested. God's perfect will taught me to be obedient because He wanted to save me from myself. His will and plans for my life led me back to my great-grandparents in their final days. There is joy in God allowing me that season.

After every downpour, God sent me back to my foundation. Every experience led me back to my great-grandparents' home. There was no place like home. Being there as a young-minded lady, I thought I was a disgrace to everyone because I was not what I planned to be. It was embarrassing to return and see my ex getting married when I had nothing to show for my stay in California. I was supposed to be a household name that would help my great-grandparents, but they always became my rock. They continuously led me back to God and my position as a preacher. The Davis residence was more than I thought it would ever be for me. It was the place where the actual version of Chantel existed—the woman who was loved as herself. I had nothing, and no one rolled an eye. They were happy I was healthy and able to keep going. God worked on my heart, mind, and soul. He told me who I was created to be, and all roads brought me to him.

After my great-grandmother's death, I sat on my bed and reminisced about the good times and the bad. All the material possessions I fought so hard to obtain meant nothing. I lost days with her and other supportive members by battling for a luxurious lifestyle. Atlanta was my wealthiest place, but I was void of God and family. I saw her there when I went to the kitchen and looked at the sink. Simple things like washing my great-grandmother's hair and sharing meals over stories filled my heart. I may have been burned out at times taking care of her, but my love and respect for her made every day a blessing. Seeing my great-grandfather's chair, I saw myself gleaning from his wisdom for years.

Giving a eulogy at my great-grandmother's service was heart-breaking. I faced the reality of her being with the true and living God. I was returning to the pulpit after four years of running. I was letting God use me as a willing vessel. I forgave the people who left me and talked about me, which changed my heart posture. Every storm was tailored and made for me, just as your storms were created for you. God knows what you're capable of as you go through the storms. Realize the only limitations you have are the ones you place on yourself. As storms pass by, redefine your boundaries and build your faith. An approaching storm can create chaos, but peace is found when you emerge from the eye of the storm. For instance, in Matthew 14:28 when Peter saw Jesus walking on water, Peter said, "'Lord, if it's you, let me come to you.'" Peter stepped out but began to doubt and started to sink.

Would you have doubted? I did. Doubt was my reaction in most of my storms. The silver lining was Jesus reaching out His hand to catch Peter, just as Christ reaches out for you and me.

He said to Peter, "'You have little faith. Why do you doubt, how often we have taken our eyes off God in a storm?'"

Why did Peter start to sink? Distraction. It's so easy to get distracted and thrown right to left by doubt and fear. The fear of the new, old, or making the wrong decisions. Doubting yourself worth and value. If you push past those feelings, the most remarkable things are on the other side of the storm when you focus on God. Revelation and elevation are waiting for you there. Our paths become rocky because we get too far from where we should be, and storms appear to redirect us to our purpose. That was the case in many of my storms. I went to Los Angeles alone as a teenager and had no idea that weeks later I would be escaping sex trafficking. Often we ask God why He allows certain things to happen in our lives, but there is no testimony without a test. We see starting over as a failure, but it's doing the same thing with new experience. Get up, brush yourself off, and learn from your mistakes. It was a lesson, not a failure. Present yourself again in a new way, and this time you will win.

Remember, no matter what storms you have encountered, scripture states that God has not given us a spirit of fear but power, love, and a sound mind (2 Timothy 1:7). The homelessness I experienced allowed me to never take a roof over my head for granted. The domestic violence made me appreciate when I found a loving partner, and the rainy days made me understand when the sun came out. I was a better person because of what I went through. The storms closed doors and put me back on the highway of purpose. Storms were not new to me. I dealt with familial storms my entire life, but I learned how to navigate them better with age. First, it was my parents, my grandparents, and then my great-grandparents. My protection from the storms was always Christ Jesus.

Never sacrifice your morals or who you are for anything or anyone. Cars, money, and houses can become idols if you let them. You will worship them instead of God. Make sure you retain and maintain them. I could have continued with the record executives to become famous, but I would have been poisoning those I was meant to influence due to my disobedience in wanting to be famous. What if they didn't make me famous? I would have destroyed my image and the principles I stood on trying to climb a ladder that wasn't mine. The storm of God's power over man's power kept coming up.

My life is the best testimony I can ever offer you. If you can see yourself in any facet of my life, learn the lessons. I was able to help take care of my grandma and do well in school at a young age. My great-grandparents loved me. As soon as I could leave home, I went as far away as possible to pursue a dream based on being an extra in a film while my other friends stayed closer to home in New York. Without proper financial literacy, support, and wisdom, I was led astray and placed in demeaning situations. I created my roadmap to success. When it took a wrong turn, I packed up and tried again. With financial literacy, support, and wisdom this time, I went to New York and Atlanta. I had a strategy and could live and do better. I had everything I needed and was never homeless again. Can I tell you when things turned out the best for me? It was when I stopped following my agenda and followed the blueprints of heaven.

Every storm was heaven-sent. God told me as a young girl what I was supposed to do. Running away led me everywhere, but I was safe in His arms. My great-grandparents were the reminders of where I was supposed to be. I would return to God and get back into my word and church. It was hard because the fast life was calling me. When you think of babies, they are in the learning stage when they are first born. Shiny things cause them to be distracted. When you are a baby in Christ, that's what happens. The allure of the shiny nightlife, flashy cars, and homes attracted me. Living at my family's home and serving God compared to my friends in big cities having their own life hurt me. Reading my word and trusting God was boring when all I could see were the things I didn't have. My vision was cloudy because of the comparison. God had to show me He had everything I would ever need. People, places, and things are fickle, but He isn't. I lost my job during the pandemic, but God still provided. I lost my great-grandparents, but God still loves me. God is doing all this in your life to let you know you may be off course, but He will get you through.

Life changes after the storm, so we must trust God. Miracles and blessings occur, and doors will open and close, but God stays the same. He remained faithful even when I wasn't. You don't need fancy or eloquent words to talk to God, as Matthew 6:8 says: "He knows what we need before we ask." I urge anyone who reads this book never to underestimate the power of prayer. When in a storm, I encourage you to reach out to the one who cares when it seems no one else does. No prayer is wasted, and no storm is without reason. I pray for every reader that you come to know the God who loves you no matter the mistakes you've made, the sins you've committed, or the times you've failed. Nothing can separate us from the love of God, no matter how many lies the enemy tells us. You will make it after the storm.

About the Author

Reverend Chantel Dean is an author and a licensed preacher and activist from Washington, D. C. She is deeply committed to the work of the Lord and loves encouraging and inspiring others. Forever a student of scripture, she has studied Christianity through its sacred texts at Harvard and Western Christianity at Yale. She is dedicated to becoming a Proverbs 31 woman and preaching and teaching biblical principles to those who need them most.

CONNECT WITH CHANTEL DEAN ON SOCIAL MEDIA

INSTAGRAM @REVCHANTELDEAN

www.ingramcontent.com/pod-product-compliance
Lightning Source LLC
Chambersburg PA
CBHW072114050526
44107CB00098BA/183